F. Anstey

Mr. Punch's Pocket Ibsen

A Collection of some of the Master's Best-Known Dramas

F. Anstey

Mr. Punch's Pocket Ibsen
A Collection of some of the Master's Best-Known Dramas

ISBN/EAN: 9783337217723

Printed in Europe, USA, Canada, Australia, Japan

Cover: Foto ©Thomas Meinert / pixelio.de

More available books at **www.hansebooks.com**

MR. PUNCH'S POCKET IBSEN

MR. PUNCH'S POCKET IBSEN

A COLLECTION OF SOME OF THE MASTER'S BEST-KNOWN DRAMAS

CONDENSED, REVISED, AND SLIGHTLY
RE-ARRANGED FOR THE BENEFIT OF THE
EARNEST STUDENT

BY

F. ANSTEY

AUTHOR OF "VICE VERSA," "VOCES POPULI," ETC.

WITH ....

LONDON
WILLIAM HEINEMANN
1893

PREFATORY NOTE

The concluding piece, " Pill-Doctor Herdal," is, as the observant reader will instantly perceive, rather a reverent attempt to tread in the footprints of the Norwegian dramatist, than a version of any actually existing master-piece. The author is conscious that his imitation is pain-fully lacking in the mysterious obscurity of the original, that the vein of allegorical symbolism is thinner through-out than it should be, and that the characters are not nearly so mad as persons invariably are in real life— but these are the faults inevitable to a prentice hand, and he trusts that due allowances may be made for them by the critical.

In conclusion he wishes to express his acknowledgments to Messrs. Bradbury and Agnew for their permission to reprint the present volume, the contents of which made their original appearance in the pages of " Punch."

CONTENTS

ROSMERSHÖLM

A

ROSMERSHÖLM

ACT FIRST

Sitting-room at Rosmershölm, with a stove, flower-stand, windows, ancient and modern ancestors, doors, and everything handsome about it. REBECCA WEST *is sitting knitting a large antimacassar which is nearly finished. Now and then she looks out of a window, and smiles and nods expectantly to someone outside.* MADAM HELSETH *is laying the table for supper.*

REBECCA.

[*Folding up her work slowly.*] But tell me precisely, what about this white horse?   [*Smiling quietly.*

Madam Helseth.

Lord forgive you, Miss !—[*fetching cruet-stand, and placing it on table*]—but you're making fun of me !

Rebecca.

[*Gravely.*] No, indeed. Nobody makes fun at Rosmersholm. Mr. Rosmer would not understand it. [*Shutting window.*] Ah, here is Rector Kroll. [*Opening door.*] You will stay to supper, will you not, Rector, and I will tell them to give us some little extra dish.

Kroll.

[*Hanging up his hat in the hall.*] Many thanks. [*Wipes his boots.*] May I come in ? [*Comes in, puts down his stick, sits down, and looks about him.*] And how do you and Rosmer get on together, eh ?

Rebecca.

Ever since your sister, Beata, went ¯mad and jumped into the mill-race, we have been as happy as two little birds together. [*After a pause, sitting down in arm-chair.*] So you don t really mind my living here all alone with Rosmer? We were afraid you might, perhaps.

KROLL.

Why, how on earth—on the contrary, I shouldn't object at all if you—[*looks at her meaningly*]—h'm!

REBECCA.

[*Interrupting, gravely.*] For shame, Rector; how can you make such jokes?

KROLL.

[*As if surprised.*] Jokes! We do not joke in these parts—but here is Rosmer.

[*Enter* ROSMER, *gently and softly.*

ROSMER.

So, my dear old friend, you have come again, after a year's absence. [*Sits down.*] We almost thought that——

KROLL.

[*Nods.*] So Miss West was saying—but you are quite mistaken. I merely thought I might remind you, if I came, of our poor Beata's suicide, so I kept away. We Norwegians are not without our simple tact.

ROSMER.

It was considerate—but unnecessary. Reb — I *mean*, Miss West—and I often allude to the incident, do we not?

REBECCA.

[*Strikes Tändstickor.*] Oh yes, indeed. [*Lighting lamp.*] Whenever we feel a little more cheerful than usual.

KROLL.

You dear good people! [*Wanders up the room.*] I came because the Spirit of Revolt has crept into my School. A Secret Society has existed for weeks in the Lower Third! To-day it has come to my knowledge that a booby trap was prepared for me by the hand of my own son, Laurits, and I then discovered that a hair had been inserted in my cane by my daughter Hilda! The only way in which a right-minded Schoolmaster can combat this anarchic and subversive spirit is to start a newspaper, and I thought that you, as a weak, credulous, inexperienced and impressionable kind of man, were the very person to be the Editor.

[REBECCA *laughs softly, as if to herself.*
ROSMER *jumps up and sits down again.*

REBECCA.

[*With a look at Rosmer.*] Tell him now!

ROSMER.

[*Returning the look.*] I can't—Some other evening. Well, perhaps—— [*To* KROLL.] I can't be your Editor — because [*in a low voice*] I—I am on the side of Laurits and Hilda!

KROLL.

[*Looks from one to the other, gloomily.*] H'm!

ROSMER.

Yes. Since we last met, I have changed my views.
I am going to create a new democracy, and awaken it
to its true task of making all the people of this
country noblemen, by freeing their wills, and
purifying their minds!

KROLL.

What *do* you mean!   [*Takes up his hat.*

ROSMER.

[*Bowing his head.*] I don't quite know, my dear
friend; it was Reb—— I should say Miss West's
scheme.

KROLL.

H'm! [*A suspicion appears in his face.*] Now I
begin to believe that what Beata said about schemes
——no matter. But under the circumstances, I will
not stay to supper.

            [*Takes up his stick, and walks out.*

Rosmer.

I *told* you he would be annoyed. I shall go to bed now. I don't want any supper. [*He lights a candle, and goes out; presently his footsteps are heard overhead, as he undresses.* Rebecca *pulls a bell-rope.*

Rebecca.

[*To* Madam Helseth, *who enters with dishes.*] No, Mr. Rosmer will not have supper to-night. [*In a lighter tone.*] Perhaps he is afraid of the nightmare. There are so many sorts of White Horses in this world!

Madam Helseth.

[*Shaking.*] Lord! lord! that Miss West—the things she does say!

> [Rebecca *goes out through door, knitting antimacassar thoughtfully, as Curtain falls.*

ACT SECOND

ROSMER'S *study. Doors and windows, bookshelves, a writing-table. Door, with curtain, leading to* ROSMER'S *bedroom.* ROSMER *discovered in a smoking jacket cutting a pamphlet with a paper-knife. There is a knock at the door.* ROSMER *says " Come in."* REBECCA *enters in a morning wrapper and curl-papers. She sits on a chair close to* ROSMER, *and looks over his shoulder as he cuts the leaves.* RECTOR KROLL *is shown up.*

KROLL.

[*Lays his hat on the table and looks at* REBECCA *from head to foot.*] I am really afraid that I am in the way.

REBECCA.

[*Surprised.*] Because I am in my morning wrapper and curl-papers? You forget that I am *emancipated*, Rector Kroll.

[*She leaves them and listens behind curtain in* ROSMER'S *bedroom.*

ROSMER.

Yes, Miss West and I have worked our way forward in faithful comradeship.

KROLL.

[*Shakes his head at him slowly.*] So I perceive. Miss West is naturally inclined to be forward. But, I say, *really* you know—— However, I came to tell you that poor Beata was not so mad as she looked, though flowers *did* bewilder her so. [*Taking off his gloves meaningly.*] She jumped into the mill-race because she had an idea that you ought to marry Miss West!

Rosmer.

[*Jumps half up from his chair.*] I ? Marry—Miss West ! My good gracious, Kroll ! I don't *understand*, it is *most* incomprehensible. [*Looks fixedly before him.*] How *can* people ?—— [*Looks at him for a moment, then rises.*] Will you get out ? [*Still quiet and self-restrained.*] But first tell me why you never mentioned this before ?

Kroll.

Why ? Because I thought you were both orthodox, which made all the difference. Now I know that you side with Laurits and Hilda, and mean to make the democracy into noblemen, and accordingly I intend to make it hot for you in my paper. *Good* morning !

> [*He slams the door with spite as* Rebecca *enters from bed-room.*

Rosmer.

[*As if surprised.*] You—in my bedroom ! You have been listening, dear ? But you *are* so emancipated.

"Taking off his gloves meaningly."

Ah, well! so our pure and beautiful friendship has been misinterpreted, bespattered! Just because you wear a morning wrapper, and have lived here alone for a year, people with coarse souls and ignoble eyes make unpleasant remarks! But what really *did* drive Beata mad? *Why* did she jump into the mill-race? I'm sure we did everything we could to spare her! I made it the business of my life to keep her in ignorance of all our interests—*didn't* I, now?

REBECCA.

You did. But why brood over it? What *does* it matter? Get on with your great beautiful task, dear —[*approaching him cautiously from behind*]—winning over minds and wills, and creating noblemen, you know—*joyful* noblemen!

ROSMER.

[*Walking about restlessly, as if in thought.*] Yes, I know. I have never laughed in the whole course of my life—we Rosmers don't—and so I felt that

spreading gladness and light, and making the democracy joyful, was properly my mission.   But *now*—I
feel too upset to go on, Rebecca, unless—— [*Shakes
his head heavily.*] Yes, an idea has just occurred to
me—— [*Looks at her, and then runs his hands through
his hair*]—Oh, my goodness ! No—I *can't.*

[*He leans his elbows on table.*

REBECCA.

Be a free man to the full, Rosmer—tell me your
idea.

ROSMER.

[*Gloomily.*] I don't know what you'll say to it.
It's this : Our platonic comradeship was all very
well while I was peaceful and happy. Now that I
am bothered and badgered, I feel—*why,* I can't
exactly explain, but I *do* feel that I must oppose a
new and living reality to the gnawing memories of
the past. I should perhaps, explain that this is
equivalent to an Ibsenian proposal.

Rebecca.

[*Catches at the chairback with joy.*] How? at *last*— a rise at last! [*Recollects herself.*] But what am I about? Am I not an emancipated enigma? [*Puts her hands over her ears as if in terror.*] What are you saying? You mustn't. I can't *think* what you mean. Go away, do!

Rosmer.

[*Softly.*] Be the new and living reality. It is the only way to put Beata out of the Saga. Shall we try it?

Rebecca.

Never! Do not—*do* not ask me why—for I haven't a notion—but never! [*Nods slowly to him and rises.*] White Horses would not induce me! [*With her hand on door-handle.*] Now you *know*! [*She goes out!*

Rosmer.

[*Sits up, stares, thunderstruck, at the stove, and says to himself.*] Well—I—am——

Quick Curtain.

B

ACT THIRD

*Sitting-room at Rosmersölm. Sun shining outside
in the Garden. Inside* REBECCA WEST *is water-
ing a geranium with a small watering-pot.
Her crochet antimacassar lies in the arm-chair.*
MADAME HELSETH *is rubbing the chairs with
furniture-polish from a large bottle. Enter*
ROSMER, *with his hat and stick in his hand.*
MADAME HELSETH *corks the bottle and goes out
to the right.*

REBECCA.

Good morning, dear. [*A moment after—crocheting.*]
Have you seen Rector Kroll's paper this morning?
There's something about *you* in it.

ROSMER.

Oh, indeed? [*Puts down hat and stick, and takes*

up paper]. H'm! [*Reads—then walks about the room.*]
Kroll *has* made it hot for me. [*Reads some more.*]
Oh, this is *too* bad! Rebecca, they *do* say such nasty
spiteful things! they actually call me a renegade—
and I can't *think* why! They *mustn't* go on like this.
All that is good in human nature will go to ruin if
they're allowed to attack an excellent man like me!
Only think, if I can make them see how unkind they
have been!

REBECCA.

Yes, dear, in that you have a great and glorious
object to attain—and I wish you may get it!

ROSMER.

Thanks. I think I shall. [*Happens to look through
window and jumps.*] Ah, no, I shan't—never now,
I have just seen——

REBECCA.

Not the White Horse, dear? We must really not
overdo that White Horse!

ROSMER.

No—the mill-race, where Beata——[*Puts on his hat
—takes it off again.*] I'm beginning to be haunted by
—no, I *don't* mean the Horse—by a terrible suspicion
that Beata may have been right after all! Yes, I do
believe, now I come to think of it, that I must really
have been in love with you from the first. Tell me
your opinion.

REBECCA.

[*Struggling with herself, and still crocheting.*] Oh
—I can't exactly say—such an odd question to ask
me!

ROSMER.

[*Shakes his head.*] Perhaps; I have no sense of
humour—no respectable Norwegian *has*—and I *do*
want to know—because, you see, if I *was* in love
with you, it was a *sin*, and if I once convinced myself
of that——

[*Wanders across the room.*

REBECCA

[*Breaking out.*] Oh, these old ancestral prejudices! Here is your hat, and your stick, too; go and take a walk.

> [ROSMER *takes hat and stick, first, then goes out and takes a walk; presently* MADAM HELSETH *appears, and tells* REBECCA *something.* REBECCA *tells her something. They whisper together.* MADAM HELSETH *nods, and shows in* RECTOR KROLL, *who keeps his hat in his hand, and sits on a chair.*

KROLL.

I merely called for the purpose of informing you that I consider you an artful and designing person, but that, on the whole, considering your birth and moral antecedents, you know—[*nods at her*]—it is not surprising. [REBECCA *walks about wringing her hands.*] Why, what *is* the matter? Did you really not know that you had no right to your father's name? I'd no *idea* you would mind my mentioning such a trifle!

KEBECCA.

[*Breaking out.*] I *do* mind. I am an emancipated enigma, but I retain a few little prejudices still. I *don't* like owning to my real age, and I *do* prefer to be legitimate. And, after your information—of which I was quite ignorant, as my mother, the late Mrs. Gamvik, never *once* alluded to it—I feel I must confess everything. Strong-minded advanced women are like that. Here is Rosmer. [ROSMER *enters with his hat and stick.*] Rosmer, I want to tell you and Rector Kroll a little story. Let us sit down, dear, all three of us. [*They sit down, mechanically, on chairs.*] A long time ago, before the play began—[*in a voice scarcely audible*]—in Ibsenite dramas, all the interesting things somehow *do* happen before the play begins——

Rosmer.

But, Rebecca, I *know* all this.

Kroll.

[*Looks hard at her.*] Perhaps I had better go?

Rebecca.

No—I will be short· This was it. I wanted to take my share in the life of the New Era, and march onward with Rosmer. There was one dismal, insurmountable barrier—[*to* Rosmer, *who nods gravely*]— Beata! I understood where your deliverance lay— and I acted. *I* drove Beata into the mill-race. . . . There!

Rosmer.

[*After a short silence*]. H'm! Well, Kroll—[*takes up his hat*]—if you're thinking of walking home, I'll go too. I'm going to be orthodox once more—after *this!*

Kroll.

[*Severely and impressively, to* Rebecca.] A nice sort of young woman *you* are! [*Both go out hastily, without looking at* Rebecca.

Rebecca.

[*Speaks to herself, under her breath.*] Now I *have* done it. I wonder *why*. [*Pulls bell-rope.*] Madam Helseth, I have just had a glimpse of two rushing White Horses. Bring down my hair-trunk.

> [*Enter* Madam Helseth, *with large hair-trunk, as Curtain falls.*

ACT FOUR

Late evening. REBECCA WEST *stands by a lighted lamp,*
with a shade over it, packing sandwiches, &c., in a
reticule, with a faint smile. The antimacassar is
on the sofa. Enter ROSMER.

ROSMER.

[*Seeing the sandwiches, &c.*] Sandwiches? Then
you *are* going! Why, on earth—I *can't* understand!

REBECCA.

Dear, you never *can.* Rosmershölm is too much
for me. But how did you get on with Kroll?

ROSMER.

We have made it up. He has convinced me that
the work of ennobling men was several sizes too large
for me—so I am going to let it alone——

Rebecca.

[*With her faint smile.*] There I almost think, dear, that you are wise.

Rosmer.

[*As if annoyed.*] What, so *you* don't believe in me either, Rebecca—you never *did !*

[*Sits listlessly on chair.*

Rebecca.

Not much, dear, when you are left to yourself—but I've another confession to make.

Rosmer.

What, *another ?* I really can't stand any more confessions just now !

Rebecca.

[*Sitting close to him.*] It is only a little one. I bullied Beata into the mill-race—because of a wild uncontrollable—— [Rosmer *moves uneasily.*] Sit still, dear—uncontrollable fancy—for *you !*

ROSMER.

[*Goes and sits on sofa.*] Oh, my goodness, Rebecca
—you *mustn't*, you know !

[*He jumps up and down as if embarrassed.*

REBECCA.

Don't be alarmed, dear, it is all over now. After
living alone with you in solitude, when you showed
me all your thoughts without reserve—little by little,
somehow the fancy passed off. I caught the Rosmer
view of life badly, and dulness descended on my soul
as an extinguisher upon one of our Northern dips.
The Rosmer view of life is ennobling, very—but hardly
lively. And I've more yet to tell you.

ROSMER.

[*Turning it off.*] Isn't that enough for one evening ?

REBECCA.

[*Almost voiceless.*] No, dear. I have a Past—*behind*
me !

ROSMER.

Behind you? How strange. I had an idea of that sort already. [*Starts, as if in fear.*] A joke! [*Sadly.*] Ah, no—*no*, I must not give way to *that!* Never mind the Past, Rebecca; I once thought that I had made the grand discovery that, if one is only virtuous, one will be happy. I see now it was too daring, too original—an immature dream. What bothers me is that I can't—somehow I *can't*—believe entirely in you—I am not even sure that I *have* ennobled you so very much—*isn't* it terrible?

REBECCA.

[*Wringing her hands.*] Oh, this killing doubt! [*Looks darkly at him.*] Is there anything *I* can do to convince you?

ROSMER.

[*As if impelled to speak against his will.*] Yes, one thing—only I'm afraid you wouldn't see it in the same light. And yet I must mention it. It is like this.

" Oh, my goodness, Rebecca—you *mustn't*, you know ! "

I want to recover faith in my mission, in my power to ennoble human souls. And, as a logical thinker, this I cannot do now, unless—well, unless you jump into the mill-race, too, like Beata!

REBECCA.

[*Takes up her antimacassar, with composure, and puts it on her head.*] Anything to oblige you.

ROSMER.

[*Springs up.*] What? You really *will!* You are *sure* you don't mind? Then, Rebecca, I will go further. I will even go—yes—as far as you go yourself!

REBECCA.

[*Bows her head towards his breast.*] You will see me off? Thanks. Now you are indeed an Ibsenite.

[*Smiles almost imperceptibly.*

ROSMER.

[*Cautiously.*] I said as far as *you* go. I don't commit myself further than that. Shall we go?

REBECCA.

First tell me this.   Are *you* going with *me*, or am *I* going with *you*?

ROSMER.

A subtle psychological point—but we have not time to think it out here.   We will discuss it as we go along.   Come!

[ROSMER *takes his hat and stick,* REBECCA *her reticule, with sandwiches.   They go out hand-in-hand through the door, which they leave open.   The room* (*as is not uncommon with rooms in Norway*) *is left empty.   Then* MADAM HELSETH *enters through another door.*

MADAM HELSETH.

The cab, Miss—not here! [*Looks out.*] Out together—at this time of night—upon my—*not* on the garden seat? [*Looks out of window.*] My goodness! *what* is that white thing on the bridge—the *Horse* at last! [*Shrieks aloud.*] And those two sinful creatures running home!

Enter ROSMER *and* REBECCA, *out of breath.*

ROSMER.

[*Scarcely able to get the words out.*] It's no use, Rebecca—we must put it off till another evening. We can't be expected to jump off a footbridge which already has a White Horse on it. And if it comes to that, why should we jump at all? I know now that I really *have* ennobled you, which was all *I* wanted. What would be the good of recovering faith in my mission at the bottom of a mill-pond? No, Rebecca— [*Lays his hand on her head*]—there is no judge over us, and therefore——

REBECCA.

[*Interrupting gravely.*] We will bind ourselves over in our own recognisances to come up for judgment when called upon.

> [MADAM HELSETH *holds on to a chair-back.*
> REBECCA *finishes the antimacassar calmly
> as Curtain falls.*

NORA; OR, THE BIRD-CAGE

(ET DIKKISVÖET)

NORA; OR, THE BIRD-CAGE
(ET DIKKISVÖET)

ACT FIRST

A room tastefully filled with cheap Art-furniture. Gimcracks in an étagere: a festoon of chenille monkeys hanging from the gaselier. Japanese fans, skeletons, cotton-wool spiders, frogs and lizards, scattered everywhere about. Drain-pipes with tall dyed grasses. A porcelain stove decorated with transferable pictures. Showily-bound books in book-case. Window. The Visitor's bell rings in the hall outside. The hall-door is heard to open, and then to shut. Presently Nora *walks in with parcels ; a porter carries a large Christmas-*

tree after her—which he puts down. NORA *gives
him a shilling—and he goes out grumbling.*
NORA *hums contentedly, and eats macaroons. Then*
HELMER *puts his head out of his Manager's room,
and* NORA *hides macaroons cautiously.*

HELMER.

[*Playfully.*] Is that my little squirrel twittering—
that my lark frisking in here ?

NORA.

Ess ! [*To herself.*] I have only been married eight
years, so these marital amenities have not yet had
time to pall !

HELMER.

[*Threatening with his finger.*] I hope the little bird
has surely not been digging its beak into any
macaroons, eh ?

NORA.

[*Bolting one, and wiping her mouth.*] No, most
certainly not. [*To herself.*] The worst of being so

babyish is—one *does* have to tell such a lot of tara-diddles! [*To* HELMER.] See what *I*'ve bought—it's been *such* fun! [*Hums.*

HELMER.

[*Inspecting parcels.*] H'm—rather an *expensive* little lark! [*Takes her playfully by the ear.*

NORA.

Little birds like to have a flutter occasionally. Which reminds me—— [*Plays with his coat-buttons.*] I'm such a simple ickle sing—but if you *are* thinking of giving me a Christmas present, make it cash!

HELMER.

Just like your poor father, *he* always asked me to make it cash—he never made any himself! It's heredity, I suppose. Well—well!

[*Goes back to his Bank.* NORA *goes on humming.*

Enter Mrs. Linden, *doubtfully.*

Nora.

What, Christina—why, how old you look! But
then you are poor. I'm not. Torvald has just been
made a Bank Manager. [*Tidies the room.*] Isn't it
really wonderfully delicious to be well off? But of
course, you wouldn't know. *We* were poor once, and,
do you know, when Torvald was ill, I—[*tossing her
head*]—though I *am* such a frivolous little squirrel,
and all that, I actually borrowed £300 for him to go
abroad. Wasn't *that* clever? Tra-la-la! I shan't
tell you *who* lent it. I didn't even tell Torvald. I
am such a mere baby I don't tell him everything.
I tell Dr. Rank, though. Oh, I'm so awfully happy
I should like to shout, " Dash it all ! "

Mrs. Linden.

[*Stroking her hair.*] Do—it is a natural and
innocent outburst—you are such a child! But I am

a widow, and want employment. *Do* you think your husband could find me a place as clerk in his Bank ? [*Proudly.*] I am an excellent knitter!

NORA.

That would really be awfully funny. [*To* HELMER, *who enters.*] Torvald, this is Christina ; she wants to be a clerk in your Bank—*do* let her! She thinks such a lot of *you.* [*To herself.*] Another taradiddle !

HELMER.

She is a sensible woman, and deserves encouragement. Come along, Mrs. Linden, and we'll see what we can do for you.

> [*He goes out through the hall with* MRS. LINDEN, *and the front-door is heard to slam after them.*

NORA.

[*Opens door, and calls.*] Now, Emmy, Ivar, and Bob, come in and have a romp with Mamma—we will play hide-and-seek. [*She gets under the table,*

smiling in quiet satisfaction; KROGSTAD *enters*—NORA
pounces out upon him.] Boo! . . . Oh, I *beg* your
pardon. I don't do this kind of thing *generally*—
though I may be a little silly.

KROGSTAD.

[*Politely.*] Don't mention it. I called because I
happened to see your husband go out with Mrs.
Linden—from which, being a person of considerable
penetration, I infer that he is about to give her my
post at the Bank. Now, as you owe me the balance
of £300, for which I hold your acknowledgment,
you will see the propriety of putting a stop to this
little game at once.

NORA.

But I don't at all—not a little wee bit! I'm so
childish, you know—why *should* I?

[*Sitting upright on carpet.*

KROGSTAD.

I will try to make it plain to the meanest capacity.
When you came to me for the loan, I naturally

" Boo ! "

required some additional security. Your father, being a shady Government official, without a penny—for, if he had possessed one, he would presumably have left it to you—without a penny, then—I, as a cautious man of business, insisted upon having his signature as a surety. Oh, we Norwegians are sharp fellows !

Nora.

Well, you *got* papa's signature. didn't you ?

Krogstad.

Oh, I *got* it right enough. Unfortunately, it was dated three days after his decease—now, how do you account for *that ?*

Nora.

How ? Why, as poor Papa was dead, and couldn't sign, I signed *for* him, that's all ! Only somehow I forgot to put the date back. *That's* how. Didn't I *tell* you I was a silly, unbusiness like little thing? It's very simple.

KROGSTAD.

Very—but what you did amounts to forgery, notwithstanding. I happen to know, because I'm a lawyer, and have done a little in the forging way myself. So, to come to the point—if *I* get kicked out, I shall not go alone!   [*He bows, and goes out.*

NORA.

It *can't* be wrong! Why, no one but Krogstad would have been taken in by it! If the Law says it's wrong, the Law's a goose—a bigger goose than poor little me even! [*To* HELMER, *who enters.*] Oh, Torvald, how you made me jump!

HELMER.

Has anybody called? [NORA *shakes her head.*] Oh, my little squirrel mustn't tell naughty whoppers Why, I just met that fellow Krogstad in the hall. He's been asking you to get me to take him back— now, hasn't he?

NORA.

[*Walking about.*] Do just see how pretty the Christmas-tree looks !

HELMER.

Never mind the tree—I want to have this out about Krogstad. I can't take him back, because many years ago he forged a name. As a lawyer, a close observer of human nature, and a Bank Manager, I have remarked that people who forge names seldom or never confide the fact to their children—which inevitably brings moral contagion into the entire family. From which it follows, logically, that Krogstad has been poisoning his children for years by acting a part, and is morally lost. [*Stretches out his hands to her.*] I can't bear a morally lost Bank-cashier about me !

NORA.

But you never thought of dismissing him till Christina came !

Helmer.

H'm ! I've got some business to attend to—so good-bye, little lark ! [*Goes into office and shuts door.*

Nora.

[*Pale with terror.*] If Krogstad poisons his children because he once forged a name, I must be poisoning Emmy, and Bob, and Ivar, because *I* forged papa's signature ! [*Short pause ; she raises her head proudly.*] After all, if I *am* a doll, I can still draw a logical inference ! I mustn't play with the children any more—[*hotly*]—I don't care—I *shall*, though ! Who cares for Krogstad ?

> [*She makes a face, choking with suppressed tears, as Curtain falls.*

ACT SECOND

The room, with the cheap Art-furniture as before—
except that the candles on the Christmas tree have
guttered down and appear to have been lately
blown out.   The cotton-wool frogs and the chenille
monkeys are disarranged, and there are walking
things on the sofa.   NORA alone.

NORA.

[*Putting on a cloak and taking it off again.*]
Bother Krogstad!   There, I won't think of him.
I'll only think of the costume ball at Consul
Stenborg's, over-head, to-night, where I am to dance
the Tarantella all alone, dressed as a Capri fisher-

D

girl. It struck Torvald that, as I am a matron with three children, my performance might amuse the Consul's guests, and, at the same time, increase his connection at the Bank. Torvald *is* so practical. [*To* Mrs. Linden, *who comes in with a large cardboard box.*] Ah, Christina, so you have brought in my old costume? *Would* you mind, as my husband's new Cashier, just doing up the trimming for me?

Mrs. Linden.

Not at all—is it not part of my regular duties? [*Sewing.*] Don't you think, Nora, that you see a little too much of Dr. Rank?

Nora.

Oh, I *couldn't* see too much of Dr. Rank! He *is* so amusing—always talking about his complaints, and heredity, and all sorts of indescribably funny things. Go away now, dear; I hear Torvald.

[Mrs. Linden *goes. Enter* Torvald *from the Manager's room.* Nora *runs trippingly to him.*

NORA.

[*Coaxing.*] Oh, Torvald, if only you won't dismiss Krogstad, you can't think how your little lark wonld jump about and twitter.

HELMER.

The inducement would be stronger but for the fact that, as it is, the little lark is generally engaged in that particular occupation. And I really *must* get rid of Krogstad. If I didn't, people would say I was under the thumb of my little squirrel here, and then Krogstad and I knew each other in early youth; and when two people knew each other in early youth —[*a short pause*]—h'm! Besides, he *will* address me as, " I say, Torvald "—which causes me most painful emotion ! He is tactless, dishonest, familiar, and morally ruined—altogether not at all the kind of person to be a Cashier in a Bank like mine.

NORA.

But he writes in scurrilous papers—he is on the staff of the Norwegian *Punch.* If you dismiss him, he may write nasty things about *you*, as wicked people did about poor dear papa!

Helmer.

Your poor dear papa was not impeccable—far from it. I *am*—which makes all the difference. I have here a letter giving Krogstad the sack. One of the conveniences of living close to the Bank is, that I can use the housemaids as Bank-messengers. [*Goes to door and calls.*] Ellen! [*Enter parlourmaid.*] Take that letter—there is no answer. [Ellen *takes it and goes.*] That's settled—and now, Nora, as I am going to my private room, it will be a capital opportunity for you to practise the tambourine—thump away, little lark, the doors are double!

[*Nods to her and goes in, shutting door.*

Nora.

[*Stroking her face.*] How *am* I to get out of this mess? [*A ring at the visitors' bell.*] Dr. Rank's ring!

"A poor fellow with both feet in the grave is not the best
authority on the fit of silk stockings."

He shall help me out of it ! [DR. RANK *appears in doorway, hanging up his great-coat.*] Dear Dr. Rank, how *are* you ?   [*Takes both his hands.*

DR. RANK.

[*Sitting down near the stove.*] I am a miserable, hypochondriacal wretch—that's what *I* am. And why am I doomed to be dismal ? Why ? Because my father died of a fit of the blues ! *Is* that fair—I put it to *you ?*

NORA.

Do try to be funnier than *that !* See, I will show you the flesh-coloured silk tights that I am to wear to-night—it will cheer you up. But you must only look at the feet—well, you may look at the rest if you're good. *Aren't* they lovely ? Will they fit me, do you think ?

DR. RANK.

[*Gloomily.*] A poor fellow with both feet in the grave is not the best authority on the fit of silk stockings. I shall be food for worms before long—I *know* I shall !

Nora.

You mustn't really be so frivolous! Take that! [*She hits him lightly on the ear with the stockings; then hums a little.*] I want you to do me a great service, Dr. Rank. [*Rolling up stockings.*] I always liked *you.* I love Torvald most, of *course*—but, somehow, I'd rather spend my time with you—you *are* so amusing!

Rank.

If I am, can't you guess why? [*A short silence.*] Because I love you! You can't pretend you didn't know it!

Nora.

Perhaps not—but it was really too clumsy of you to mention it just as I was about to ask a favour of you! It was in the worst taste! [*With dignity.*] You must not imagine because I joke with you about silk stockings, and tell you things I never tell Torvald, that I am therefore without the most delicate and scrupulous self-respect! I am really quite a good little doll, Dr. Rank, and now—[*sits in rocking chair and smiles*]—now I shan't ask you what I was going to! [ELLEN *comes in with a card.*]

NORA.

[*Terrified.*] Oh, my goodness!

[*Puts it in her pocket.*

DR. RANK.

Excuse my easy Norwegian pleasantry—but—h'm —anything disagreeable up?

NORA.

[*To herself.*] Krogstad's card! I must tell *another* whopper! [*To* RANK.] No, nothing—only—only my new costume. I want to try it on here. I always do try on my dresses in the drawing-room—it's *cosier*, you know. So go in to Torvald and amuse him till I'm ready.

[RANK *goes into* HELMER'S *room, and* NORA
bolts the door upon him, as KROGSTAD
enters from hall in a fur cap.

Krogstad.

Well, I've got the sack, and so I came to see how *you* are getting on. I mayn't be a nice man, but— [*with feeling*]—I have a heart! And, as I don't intend to give up the forged I.O.U. unless I'm taken back, I was afraid you might be contemplating suicide, or something of that kind; and so I called to tell you that, if I were you, I wouldn't. Bad thing for the complexion, suicide—and silly, too, because it wouldn't mend matters in the least. [*Kindly.*] You must not take this affair too seriously, Mrs. Helmer. Get your husband to settle it amicably by taking me back as Cashier; *then* I shall soon get the whip-hand of *him*, and we shall all be as pleasant and comfortable as possible together!

Nora.

Not even that prospect can tempt me! Besides, Torvald wouldn't have you back at any price now!

KROGSTAD.

All right, then.   I have here a letter, telling your husband all.   I will take the liberty of dropping it in the letter-box at your hall-door as I go out.   I'll wish you good evening !

> [*He goes out; presently the dull sound of a thick letter dropping into a wire box is heard.*

NORA.

[*Softly, and hoarsely.*] He's done it !   How *am* I to prevent Torvald from seeing it ?

HELMER.

[*Inside the door, rattling.*] Hasn't my lark changed its dress yet ?   [NORA *unbolts door.*] What—so you are *not* in fancy costume, after all ?   [*Enters with* RANK.] Are there any letters for me in the box there ?

NORA.

[*Voicelessly.*] None—not even a postcard !   Oh,

Torvald, don't, please, go and look—*promise* me you won't! I do *assure* you there isn't a letter! And I've forgotten the Tarantella you taught me—do let's run over it. I'm so afraid of breaking down— promise me not to look at the letter-box. I can't dance unless you do.

HELMER.

[*Standing still, on his way to the letter-box.*] I am a man of strict business habits, and some powers of observation; my little squirrel's assurances that there is nothing in the box, combined with her obvious anxiety that I should not go and see for myself, satisfy me that it is indeed empty, in spite of the fact that I have not invariably found her a strictly truthful little dicky-bird. There—there. [*Sits down to piano.*] Bang away on your tambourine, little squirrel—dance away, my own lark!

NORA.

[*Dancing, with a long gay shawl.*] Just *won't* the little squirrel! Faster—faster! Oh, I *do* feel so gay! We will have some champagne for dinner, *won't* we, Torvald?

[*Dances with more and more abandonment.*

HELMER.

[*After addressing frequent remarks in correction.*] Come, come—not this awful wildness! I don't like to see *quite* such a larky little lark as this. . . . . . Really it is time you stopped!

NORA.

[*Her hair coming down as she dances more wildly still, and swings the tambourine.*] I can't. . . . . . I can't! [*To herself, as she dances.*] I've only thirty-one hours left to be a bird in; and after that—[*shuddering*]—after *that*, Krogstad will let the cat out of the bag!

Curtain.

ACT THIRD

*The same room—except that the sofa has been slightly
moved, and one of the Japanese cotton-wool frogs
has fallen into the fire-place.* MRS. LINDEN *sits
and reads a book—but without understanding a
single line.*

MRS. LINDEN.

[*Laying down her book, as a light tread is heard
outside.*] Here he is at last! [KROGSTAD *comes in,
and stands in the doorway.*] Mr. Krogstad, I have
given you a secret *rendezvous* in this room, because it
belongs to my employer, Mr. Helmer, who has lately
discharged you. The etiquette of Norway permits

these slight freedoms on the part of a female cashier.

KROGSTAD.

It does. Are we alone? [NORA *is heard overhead dancing the Tarantella.*] Yes, I hear Mrs. Helmer's fairy footfall above. She dances the Tarantella now—by-and-by she will dance to another tune! [*Changing his tone.*] I don't exactly know why you should wish to have this interview—after jilting me as you did, long ago, though?

MRS. LINDEN.

Don't you? *I* do. I am a widow—a Norwegian widow. And it has occurred to me that there may be a nobler side to your nature somewhere—though you have not precisely the best of reputations

KROGSTAD.

Right. I am a forger, and a money-lender; I am on the staff of the Norwegian *Punch*—a most scurrilous paper. More, I have been blackmailing

Mrs. Helmer by trading on her fears, like a low cowardly cur. But, in spite of all that—[*clasping his hands*]—there are the makings of a fine man about me *yet*, Christina !

MRS. LINDEN.

I believe you—at least, I'll chance it. I want some one to care for, and I'll marry you.

KROGSTAD.

[*Suspiciously.*] On condition, I suppose, that I suppress the letter denouncing Mrs. Helmer ?

MRS. LINDEN.

How can you think so ? I am her dearest friend ; but I can still see her faults, and it is my firm opinion that a sharp lesson will do her all the good in the world. She is *much* too comfortable. So leave the letter in the box, and come home with me.

KROGSTAD.

I am wildly happy ! Engaged to the female

cashier of the manager who has discharged me, our future is bright and secure!

> [*He goes out; and* MRS. LINDEN *sets the furniture straight; presently a noise is heard outside, and* HELMER *enters, dragging* NORA *in. She is in fancy dress, and he in an open black domino.*

NORA.

I shan't! It's too early to come away from such a nice party. I *won't* go to bed! [*She whimpers.*

HELMER.

[*Tenderly.*] There'sh a naughty lil' larkie for you, Mrs. Linen! Poshtively had to drag her 'way! She'sh a capricious lil' girl—from Capri. 'Scuse me! —'fraid I've been and made a pun. Shan' 'cur again! Shplendid champagne the Consul gave us— 'counts for it! [*Sits down smiling.*] Do you *knit*, Mrs. Cotton? . . . . You shouldn't. Never knit. 'Broider. [*Nodding to her, solemnly.*] 'Member that.

E

Alwaysh *'broider*.   More—[*hiccoughing*] — Oriental !
Gobblesh you !—goo'ni !

Mrs. Linden.

I only came in to—to see Nora's costume.   Now
I've seen it, I'll go.   [*Goes out.*

Helmer.

Awful bore that woman—hate boresh !   [*Looks at*
Nora, *then comes nearer.*] Oh, you prillil squillikins,
I *do* love you so !   Shomehow, I feel sho lively
thishevenin' !

Nora.

[*Goes to other side of table.*]   I won't *have* all that,
Torvald !

Helmer.

Why ? ain't you my lil' lark—ain't thish our lil
cage ? Ver-*well*, then. [*A ring.*] Rank ! confound
it all ! [*Enter* Dr. Rank.] Rank, dear old boy,
you've been [*hiccoughs*] going it upstairs.   Cap'tal
champagne, eh ?   '*Shamed* of you, Rank !

[*He sits down on sofa, and closes his eyes gently.*

"Oh, you prillil squillikins!"

DR. RANK.

Did you notice it? [*With pride.*] It was almost incredible the amount I contrived to put away. But I shall suffer for it to-morrow. [*Gloomily.*] Heredity again! I wish I was dead! I do.

NORA.

Don't apologise. Torvald was just as bad; but he is always so good-tempered after champagne.

DOCTOR RANK.

Ah, well, I just looked in to say that I haven't long to live. Don't weep for me, Mrs. Helmer, it's chronic—and hereditary too. Here are my P.P.C. cards. I'm a fading flower. Can you oblige me with a cigar?

NORA.

[*With a suppressed smile.*] Certainly. Let me give you a light?

> [DOCTOR RANK *lights his cigar, after several ineffectual attempts, and goes out.*

HELMER.

[*Compassionately.*] Poo' old Rank—he'sh very bad to-ni'! [*Pulls himself together.*] But I forgot— Bishness—I mean, bu-si-ness—mush be 'tended to. I'll go and see if there are any letters. [*Goes to box.*] Hallo! some one's been at the lock with a hairpin— it's one of *your* hairpins! [*Holding it out to her.*

NORA.

[*Quickly.*] Not mine—one of Bob's, or Ivar's— they both wear hairpins!

HELMER.

[*Turning over letters absently.*] You must break them of it—bad habit! What a lot o' lettersh! *double* usual quantity. [*Opens* KROGSTAD'S.] By Jove! [*Reads it and falls back completely sobered.*] What have you got to say to *this ?*

NORA.

[*Crying aloud.*] You shan't save me—let me go! I *won't* be saved!

HELMER.

Save *you*, indeed! Who's going to save *Me?* You miserable little criminal. [*Annoyed.*] Ugh—ugh!

NORA.

[*With hardening expression.*] Indeed, Torvald, your singing-bird acted for the best!

HELMER.

Singing-bird! Your father was a rook—and you take *after* him. Heredity again! You have utterly destroyed my happiness. [*Walks round several times.*] Just as I was beginning to get on, too!

NORA.

I have—but I will go away and jump into the water.

HELMER.

What good will *that* do me? People will say *I* had a hand in this business. [*Bitterly.*] If you *must* forge, you might at least put your dates in correctly! But you never *had* any principle! [*A ring.*] The front-

door bell! [*A fat letter is seen to fall into the box ;*
HELMER *takes it, opens it, sees enclosure, and embraces*
NORA.] Krogstad won't split. See, he returns the
forged I.O.U.! Oh, my poor little lark, *what* you
must have gone through! Come under my wing, my
little scared song-bird. . . . . Eh? you *won't!*
Why, what's the matter *now?*

NORA.

[*With cold calm.*] I have wings of my own, thank
you, Torvald, and I mean to use them!

HELMER.

What—leave your pretty cage, and [*pathetically*]
the old cock bird, and the poor little innocent eggs!

NORA.

Exactly. Sit down, and we will talk it over first.
[*Slowly.*] Has it ever struck you that this is the
first time you and I have ever talked seriously
together about serious things?

HELMER.

Come, I do like that! How on earth could we talk about serious things when your mouth was always full of macaroons?

NORA.

[*Shakes her head.*] Ah, Torvald, the mouth of a mother of a family should have more solemn things in it than macaroons! I see that now, too late. No, you have wronged me. So did papa. Both of you called me a doll, and a squirrel, and a lark! You might have made something of me—and instead of that, you went and made too much of me—oh, you *did !*

HELMER.

Well, you didn't seem to object to it, and really I don't exactly see what it is you *do* want!

NORA.

No more do I—that is what I have got to find out. If I had been properly educated, I should have known better than to date poor papa's signature three days after he died. Now I must educate ·*myself.* I have to gain experience, and get clear about religion, and law, and things, and whether Society is right or I am—and I must go away and never come back any more till I *am* educated!

HELMER.

Then you may be away some little time? And what's to become of me and the eggs meanwhile?

NORA.

That, Torvald, is entirely your own affair. I have a higher duty than that towards you and the eggs. [*Looking solemnly upward.*] I mean my duty towards Myself!

HELMER.

And all this because—in a momentary annoyance at finding myself in the power of a discharged cashier who calls me "I say, Torvald," I expressed myself with ultra-Gilbertian frankness! You talk like a silly child!

NORA.

Because my eyes are opened, and I see my position with the eyes of Ibsen. I must go away at once, and begin to educate myself.

HELMER.

May I ask how you are going to set about it ?

NORA.

Certainly. I shall begin—yes, I shall *begin* with a course of the Norwegian theatres. If *that* doesn't take the frivolity out of me, I don't really know what *will !* [*She gets her bonnet and ties it tightly.*

HELMER.

Then you are really going ? And you'll never think about me and the eggs any more ! Oh, Nora !

NORA.

Indeed, I shall—occasionally—as strangers.

> [*She puts on a shawl sadly, and fetches her dressing-bag.*]

If I ever do come back, the greatest miracle of all
will have to happen.   Good-bye!

> [*She goes out through the hall; the front door
> is heard to bang loudly.*

HELMER.

[*Sinking on a chair.*] The room empty?   Then she
must be gone!   Yes, my little lark has flown! [*The
dull sound of an unskilled latchkey is heard trying
the lock; presently the door opens, and* NORA, *with a
somewhat foolish expression, reappears.*] What? back
already!   Then you *are* educated?

NORA.

[*Puts down dressing-bag.*] No, Torvald, not yet.
Only, you see, I found I had only threepence-half-
penny in my purse, and the Norwegian theatres are
all closed at this hour—and so I thought I wouldn't
leave the cage till to-morrow—after breakfast.

HELMER.

[*As if to himself.*] The greatest miracle of all *has*

happened. My little bird is not in the bush *just* yet !

> [NORA *takes down a showily-bound diction-*
> *ary from the shelf and begins her educa-*
> *tion ;* HELMER *fetches a bag of macaroons,*
> *sits near her, and tenders one humbly. A*
> *pause.* NORA *repulses it, proudly. He*
> *offers it again. She snatches at it sud-*
> *denly, still without looking at him, and*
> *nibbles it thoughtfully as Curtain falls.*

HEDDA GABLER

HEDDA GABLER

ACT FIRST

SCENE—*A sitting-room cheerfully decorated in dark colours. Broad doorway, hung with black crape, in the wall at back, leading to a back drawing-room, in which, above a sofa in black horsehair, hangs a posthumous portrait of the late* GENERAL GABLER. *On the piano is a handsome pall. Through the glass panes of the back drawing-room window are seen a dead wall and a cemetery. Settees, sofas, chairs, &c., handsomely upholstered in black bombazine, and studded with small round nails. Bouquets of immortelles and dead grasses are lying everywhere about.*

F

Enter AUNT JULIE (*a good-natured-looking lady
in a smart hat.*)

AUNT JULIE.

Well, I declare, if I believe George or Hedda are
up yet! [*Enter* GEORGE TESMAN, *humming, stout,
careless, spectacled.*] Ah, my dear boy, I have called
before breakfast to inquire how you and Hedda are
after returning late last night from your long honeymoon. Oh, dear me, yes; am I not your old aunt,
and are not these attentions usual in Norway?

GEORGE.

Good Lord, yes! My six months' honeymoon
has been quite a little travelling scholarship, eh? I
have been examining archives. Think of *that!* Look
here, I'm going to write a book all about the
domestic interests of the Cave-dwellers during the
Deluge. I'm a clever young Norwegian man of
letters, eh?

AUNT JULIE.

Fancy your knowing about that too! Now, dear me, thank Heaven!

GEORGE.

Let me, as a dutiful Norwegian nephew, untie that smart, showy hat of yours. [*Unties it, and pats her under the chin.*] Well, to be sure, you have got yourself really up—fancy that!

[*He puts hat on chair close to table.*

AUNT JULIE.

[*Giggling.*] It was for Hedda's sake—to go out walking with her in. [HEDDA *approaches from the back-room; she is pallid, with cold, open, steel-grey eyes; her hair is not very thick, but what there is of it is an agreeable medium brown.*] Ah, dear Hedda!

[*She attempts to cuddle her.*

HEDDA.

[*Shrinking back.*] Ugh, let me go, do! [*Looking at* AUNT JULIE's *hat.*] Tesman, you must really tell the housemaid not to leave her old hat about on the drawing-room chairs. Oh, is it *your* hat? Sorry I spoke, I'm sure!

AUNT JULIE.

[*Annoyed.*] Good gracious, little Mrs. Hedda; my nice new hat that I bought to go out walking with *you* in!

GEORGE.

[*Patting her on the back.*] Yes, Hedda, she did, and the parasol too! Fancy, Aunt Julie always positively thinks of everything, eh?

HEDDA.

[*Coldly.*] You hold *your* tongue. Catch me going out walking with your aunt! One doesn't *do* such things.

GEORGE.

[*Beaming.*] Isn't she a charming woman? Such fascinating manners! My goodness, eh? Fancy that!

AUNT JULIE.

Ah, dear George, you ought indeed to be happy—but [*brings out a flat package wrapped in newspaper*] look *here*, my dear boy!

GEORGE.

[*Opens it.*] What? my dear old morning shoes! my slippers! [*Breaks down.*] This is positively too touching, Hedda, eh? Do you remember how badly I wanted them all the honeymoon? Come and just have a look at them—you *may!*

HEDDA.

Bother your old slippers and your old aunt too! [AUNT JULIE *goes out annoyed, followed by* GEORGE, *still thanking her warmly for the slippers;* HEDDA *yawns;* GEORGE *comes back and places his old slippers reverently on the table.*] Why, here comes Mrs Elvsted—*another* early caller! She had irritating

hair, and went about making a sensation with it—
an old flame of yours, I've heard.

Enter MRS. ELVSTED ; *she is pretty and gentle, with
copious wavy white-gold hair and round promi-
nent eyes, and the manner of a frightened rabbit.*

MRS. ELVSTED.

[*Nervous.*] Oh, please, I'm so perfectly in despair.
Ejlert Lövborg, you know, who was our tutor ; he's
written such a large new book. I inspired him. Oh,
I know I don't look like it—but I did—he told me
so. And, good gracious! now he's in this dangerous
wicked town all alone, and he's a reformed character,
and I'm *so* frightened about him ; so, as the wife of a
sheriff twenty years older than me, I came up to
look after Mr. Lövborg. Do ask him here—then I
can meet him. You will ? How perfectly lovely of
you ! My husband's *so* fond of him !

HEDDA.

George, go and write an invitation at once; do you
hear ? [GEORGE *looks around for his slippers, takes*

them up and goes out.] Now we can talk, my little Thea. Do you remember how I used to pull your hair when we met on the stairs, and say I would scorch it off? Seeing people with copious hair always *does* irritate me.

Mrs. Elvsted.

Goodness, yes, you were always so playful and friendly, and I was so afraid of you. I am still. And please, I've run away from my husband. Everything around him was distasteful to me. And Mr. Lövborg and I were comrades—he was dissipated, and I got a sort of power over him, and he made a real person out of me—which I wasn't before, you know; but, oh, I do hope I'm real now. He talked to me and taught me to think—chiefly of him. So, when Mr. Lövborg came here, naturally I came too. There was nothing else to do! And fancy, there is another woman whose shadow still stands between him and me! She wanted to shoot him once, and so, of course, he can never forget her. I wish I knew her name—perhaps it was that red-haired opera-singer ?

HEDDA.

[*With cold self-command.*] Very likely— but nobody does that sort of thing here. Hush! Run away now. Here comes Tesman with Judge Brack. [MRS. ELVSTED *goes out;* GEORGE *comes in with* JUDGE BRACK, *who is a short and elastic gentleman, with a round face, carefully brushed hair, and distinguished profile.*] How awfully funny you do look by daylight, Judge !

BRACK.

[*Holding his hat and dropping his eye-glass.*] Sincerest thanks. Still the same graceful manners, dear little Mrs. Hed—Tesman!   I came to invite dear Tesman to a little bachelor-party to celebrate his return from his long honeymoon.   It is customary in Scandinavian society. It will be a lively affair, for I am a gay Norwegian dog.

"I am a gay Norwegian dog."

GEORGE.

Asked out—without my wife! Think of that!
Eh? Oh, dear me, yes, *I*'ll come!

BRACK.

By the way, Lövborg is here; he has written a
wonderful book, which has made a quite extraordinary
sensation. Bless me, yes!

GEORGE.

Lövborg—fancy! Well, I *am*—glad. Such mar-
vellous gifts! And I was so painfully certain he had
gone to the bad. Fancy that, eh? But what will
become of him *now*, poor fellow, eh? I *am* so anxious
to know!

BRACK.

Well, he may possibly put up for the Professorship
against you, and, though you *are* an uncommonly
clever man of letters—for a Norwegian—it's not
wholly improbable that he may cut you out!

GEORGE.

But, look here, good Lord, Judge Brack!—[*gesticulating*]—that would show an incredible want of consideration for me! I married on my chance of *getting* that professorship. A man like Lövborg, too, who hasn't even been respectable, eh? One doesn't do such things as that!

BRACK.

Really? You forget we are all realistic and unconventional persons here, and do all kinds of odd things. But don't worry yourself! [*He goes out.*

GEORGE.

[*To* HEDDA.] Oh, I say, Hedda, what's to become of our fairyland now, eh? We can't have a liveried servant, or give dinner parties, or have a horse for riding. Fancy that!

HEDDA.

[*Slowly, and wearily.*] No, we shall really have to set up as fairies in reduced circumstances, now.

GEORGE.

[*Cheering up.*] Still, we shall see Aunt Julie every day, and *that* will be something, and I've got back my old slippers. We shan't be altogether without some amusements, eh?

HEDDA.

[*Crosses the floor.*] Not while I have *one* thing to amuse myself with, at all events.

GEORGE.

[*Beaming with joy.*] Oh, Heaven be praised and thanked for that! My goodness, so you have! And what may *that* be, Hedda, eh?

HEDDA.

[*At the doorway, with suppressed scorn.*] Yes, George you have the old slippers of the attentive aunt, and I have the horse-pistols of the deceased general!

GEORGE.

[*In an agony.*] The pistols! Oh, my goodness! *what* pistols?

HEDDA.

[*With cold eyes.*] General Gabler's pistols—same which I shot—[*recollecting herself*]—no, that's Thackeray, not Ibsen—a *very* different person.

[*She goes through the back drawing-room.*

GEORGE.

[*At doorway, shouting after her.*] Dearest Hedda, *not* those dangerous things, eh? Why, they have never once been known to shoot straight yet! Don't! Have a catapult. For *my* sake, have a catapult!

[*Curtain.*

ACT SECOND

SCENE—*The cheerful dark drawing-room. It is after-noon.* HEDDA *stands loading a revolver in the back drawing-room.*

HEDDA.

[*Looking out and shouting.*] How do you do, Judge? [*Aims at him.*] Mind yourself! [*She fires.*

BRACK.

[*Entering.*] What the devil! Do you usually take pot-shots at casual visitors? [*Annoyed.*

HEDDA.

Invariably, when they come by the back-garden. It is my unconventional way of intimating that I am at home. One does do these things in realistic dramas, you know. And I was only aiming at the blue sky.

BRACK.

Which accounts for the condition of my hat. [*Exhibiting it.*] Look here—*riddled!*

HEDDA.

Couldn't help myself. I am so horribly bored with Tesman. Everlastingly to be with a professional person!

BRACK.

[*Sympathetically.*] Our excellent Tesman is certainly a bit of a bore. [*Looks searchingly at her.*] What on earth made you marry him?

HEDDA.

Tired of dancing, my dear, that's all. And then I used Tesman to take me home from parties; and we saw this villa; and I said I liked it, and so did he; and so we found some common ground, and here we are, do you see! And I loathe Tesman, and I don't even like the villa now; and I do feel the want of an entertaining companion so!

BRACK.

Try me. Just the kind of three-cornered arrangement that I like. Let me be the third person in the compartment—[*confidentially*]—the tried friend, and, generally speaking, cock of the walk!

HEDDA.

[*Audibly drawing in her breath.*] I cannot resist your polished way of putting things. We will conclude a triple alliance. But hush!—here comes Tesman.

Enter GEORGE *with a number of books under his arm.*

GEORGE.

Puff! I *am* hot, HEDDA. I've been looking into Lövborg's new book. Wonderfully thoughtful— confound him! But I must go and dress for your party, Judge. [*He goes out.*

G

HEDDA.

I wish I could get Tesman to take to politics, Judge. Couldn't he be a Cabinet Minister, or something?

BRACK.

H'm!

> [*A short pause; both look at one another, without speaking. Enter* GEORGE, *in evening dress with gloves.*

GEORGE.

It is afternoon, and your party is at half-past seven —but I like to dress early. Fancy that! And I am expecting Lövborg.

EJLERT LÖVBORG *comes in from the hall; he is worn and pale, with red patches on his cheek-bones, and wears an elegant perfectly new visiting-suit and black gloves.*

GEORGE.

Welcome! [*Introduces him to* BRACK.] Listen—I have got your new book, but I haven't read it through yet.

LÖVBORG.

You needn't—it's rubbish. [*Takes a packet of MSS. out.*] This *isn't*. It's in three parts; the first about the civilising forces of the future, the second about the future of the civilising forces, and the third about the forces of the future civilisation. I thought I'd read you a little of it this evening?

BRACK *and* GEORGE.

[*Hastily.*] Awfully nice of you—but there's a little party this evening—so sorry we can't stop! Won't you come too?

HEDDA.

No, he must stop and read it to me and Mrs. Elvsted instead.

GEORGE.

It would never have occurred to me to think of such clever things! Are you going to oppose me for the professorship, eh?

LÖVBORG.

[*Modestly.*] No; I shall only triumph over you in the popular judgment—that's all!

GEORGE.

Oh, is that all? Fancy! Let us go into the back drawing-room and drink cold punch.

LÖVBORG.

Thanks—but I am a reformed character, and have renounced cold punch—it is poison.

> [GEORGE *and* BRACK *go into the back-room
> and drink punch, whilst* HEDDA *shows*
> LÖVBORG *a photograph album in the front.*

LÖVBORG.

[*Slowly, in a low tone.*] Hedda Gabbler! how *could* you throw yourself away like this!—Oh, is *that* the Ortler Group? Beautiful!——Have you forgotten how we used to sit on the settee together behind an illustrated paper, and—yes, very picturesque peaks— I told you all about how I had been on the loose?

HEDDA.

Now, none of that here! These are the Dolomites.
—Yes, I remember; it was a beautiful fascinating
Norwegian intimacy—but it's over now. See, we
spent a night in that little mountain village, Tesman
and I.

LÖVBORG.

Did you, indeed? Do you remember that delicious
moment when you threatened to shoot me down?
[*Tenderly*] I do!

HEDDA.

[*Carelessly.*] Did I! I have done that to so many
people. But now all that is past, and you have found
the loveliest consolation in dear, good, little Mrs.
Elvsted—ah, here she is! [*Enter* MRS. ELVSTED.]
Now, Thea, sit down and drink up a good glass of
cold punch. Mr. Lövborg is going to have some. If
you don't, Mr. Lövborg, George and the Judge will
think you are afraid of taking too much if you once
begin.

Mrs. Elvsted.

Oh, please, Hedda! When I've inspired Mr. Lövborg so—good gracious! *don't* make him drink cold punch!

Hedda.

You see, Mr. Lövborg, our dear little friend can't *trust* you!

Lövborg.

So *that* is my comrade's faith in me! [*Gloomily.*] *I'll* show her if I am to be trusted or not. [*He drinks a glass of punch.*] Now I'll go to the Judge's party I'll have another glass first. Your health, Thea! So you came up to spy on me, eh? I'll drink the Sheriff's health—*everybody's* health!

[*He tries to get more punch.*

Hedda.

[*Stopping him.*] No more now. You are going to a party, remember.

George *and* Tesman *come in from back-room.*

LÖVBORG.

Don't be angry, Thea. I was fallen for a moment.
Now I'm up again! [MRS. ELSTED *beams with delight.*]
Judge, I'll come to your party, as you *are* so pressing,
and I'll read George my manuscript all the evening.
I'll do all in *my* power to make that party go!

GEORGE.

No? fancy! that *will* be amusing!

HEDDA.

There, go away, you wild rollicking creatures!
But Mr. Lövborg must be back at ten, to take dear
Thea home!

MRS. ELVSTED.

Oh, goodness, yes! [*In concealed agony.*] Mr.
Lövborg, I shan't go away till you do!

> [*The three men go out laughing merrily; the
> Act-drop is lowered for a minute; when it
> is raised, it is 7 A.M., and* MRS. ELVSTED
> *and* HEDDA *are discovered sitting up, with
> rugs around them.*

Mrs. Elvsted

[*Wearily.*] Seven in the morning, and Mr. Lövborg not here to take me home *yet!* what *can* he be doing?

Hedda.

[*Yawning.*] Reading to Tesman, with vine-leaves in his hair, I suppose. Perhaps he has got to the third part.

Mrs. Elvsted.

Oh, do you *really* think so, Hedda. Oh, if I could but hope he was doing that!

Hedda.

You silly little ninny! I should like to scorch your hair off. Go to bed!

[Mrs. Elvsted *goes. Enter* George.

George.

I'm a little late, eh? But we made *such* a night of it. Fancy! It was most amusing. Ejlert read his book to me—think of that! Astonishing book!

Oh, we really had great fun ! I wish *I'd* written it. Pity he's so irreclaimable.

HEDDA.

I suppose you mean he has more of the courage of life than most people ?

GEORGE.

Good Lord ! He had the courage to get more drunk than most people. But, altogether, it was what you might almost call a Bacchanalian orgy. We finished up by going to have early coffee with some of these jolly chaps, and poor old Lövborg dropped his precious manuscript in the mud, and I picked it up—and here it is ! Fancy if anything were to happen to it ! He never could write it again. *Wouldn't* it be sad, eh ? Don't tell any one about it.

> [*He leaves the packet of MSS. on a chair, and rushes out;* HEDDA *hides the packet as* BRACK *enters.*

BRACK.

Another early call, you see! My party was such a singularly animated *soirée* that I haven't undressed all night. Oh, it was the liveliest affair conceivable! And, like a true Norwegian host, I tracked Lövborg home; and it is only my duty, as a friend of the house, and cock of the walk, to take the first opportunity of telling you that he finished up the evening by coming to mere loggerheads with a red-haired opera-singer, and being taken off to the police-station! Your mustn't have him here any more. Remember our little triple alliance!

HEDDA.

[*Her smile fading away.*] You are certainly a dangerous person—but you must not get a hold over *me !*

BRACK.

[*Ambiguously.*] What an idea! But I might—I am an insinuating dog. Gcod morning! [*Goes out.*

LÖVBORG.

[*Bursting in, confused and excited.*] l suppose you've heard where *I've* been ?

HEDDA.

[*Evasively.*] I heard you had a very jolly party at Judge Brack's.

MRS. ELVSTED *comes in.*

LÖVBORG.

It's all over. I don't mean to do any more work. I've no use for a companion now, Thea. Go home to your sheriff!

MRS. ELVSTED.

[*Agitated.*] Never! I want to be with you when your book comes out !

LÖVBORG.

It won't *come* out—I've torn it up ! [MRS. ELSTED *rushes out, wringing her hands.*] Mrs. Tesman, I told her a lie—but no matter. I haven't torn my book up—I've done worse ! I've taken it about to several parties, and it's been through a police-row with me—now I've lost it. Even if I found it again, it wouldn't be the same—not to me! I am a Norwegian literary man, and peculiar. So I must make an end of it altogether!

HEDDA.

Quite so—but look here, you must do it beautifully. I don't insist on your putting vine-leaves in your hair—but do it beautifully. [*Fetches pistol.*] See, here is one of General Gabler's pistols—do it with *that!*

LÖVBORG.

Thanks!

> [*He takes the pistol, and goes out through the hall-door; as soon as he has gone,* HEDDA *brings out the manuscript, and puts it on the fire, whispering to herself, as Curtain falls.*

"I am a Norwegian literary man, and peculiar."

ACT THREE

SCENE.—*The same room, but—it being evening—darker than ever. The crape curtains are drawn. A servant, with black ribbons in her cap, and red eyes, comes in and lights the gas quietly and carefully. Chords are heard on the piano in the back drawing-room. Presently* HEDDA *comes in and looks out into the darkness. A short pause. Enter* GEORGE TESMAN.

GEORGE.

I am *so* uneasy about poor Lövborg. Fancy! he is not at home. Mrs. Elvsted told me he has been here early this morning, so I suppose you gave him back his manuscript, eh?

HEDDA.

[*Cold and immovable, supported by arm-chair.*] No,
I put it on the fire instead.

GEORGE.

On the fire! Lövborg's wonderful new book that
he read to me at Brack's party, when we had that
wild revelry last night! Fancy *that!* But, I say,
Hedda—isn't that *rather*—eh? *Too* bad, you know
—really. A great work like that. How on earth did
you come to think of it?

HEDDA.

[*Suppressing an almost imperceptible smile.*] Well,
dear George, you gave me a tolerably strong hint.

GEORGE.

Me? Well, to be sure—that *is* a joke! Why, I
only said that I envied him for writing such a book,
and it would put me entirely in the shade if it came
out, and if anything was to happen to it, I should

never forgive myself, as poor Lövborg couldn't write it all over again, and so we must take the greatest care of it! And then I left it on a chair and went away—that was all! And you went and burnt the book all up! Bless me, who *would* have expected it?

HEDDA.

Nobody, you dear simple old soul! But I did it for your sake—it was *love*, George!

GEORGE.

[*In an outburst between doubt and joy.*] Hedda, you don't mean that! Your love takes such queer forms sometimes. Yes, but yes—[*laughing in excess of joy*] why, you *must* be fond of me! Just think of that now! Well, you *are* fun, Hedda! Look here, I must just run and tell the housemaid that—she will enjoy the joke so, eh?

HEDDA.

[*Coldly, in self-command.*] It is surely not necessary even for a clever Norwegian man of letters in a

H

realistic social drama, to make quite such a fool of himself as all that

George.

No, that's true too. Perhaps we'd better keep it quiet—though I *must* tell Aunt Julie—it will make her so happy to hear that you burnt a manuscript on my account! And, besides, I should like to ask her whether that's a usual thing with young wives. [*Looks uneasy and pensive again.*] But poor old Ejlert's manuscript! Oh Lor', you know! Well, well!

Mrs. Elvsted comes in

Mrs. Elvsted.

Oh, please, I'm so uneasy about dear Mr. Lövborg. Something has happened to him, I'm sure!

[*Judge Brack comes in from the hall, with a new hat in his hand.*

Brack.

You have guessed it, first time. Something *has!*

Mrs. Elvsted.

Oh, dear, good gracious! What is it? Something distressing, I'm certain of it!　　　　[*Shrieks aloud.*

Brack.

[*Pleasantly.*] That depends on how one takes it. He has shot himself, and is in a hospital now, that's all!

George.

[*Sympathetically.*] That's sad, eh? poor old Lövborg! Well, I *am* cut up to hear that. Fancy, though, eh?

Hedda.

Was it through the temple, or through the breast? The breast? Well, one can do it beautifully through the breast, too, Do you know, as an advanced woman, I like an act of that sort—it's so positive to have the courage to settle the account with himself—it's beautiful, really!

Mrs. Elvsted.

Oh, Hedda, what an odd way to look at it! But never mind poor dear Mr. Lövborg now. What *we've*

got to do is to see if we can't put his wonderful
manuscript, that he said he had torn to pieces, together
again. [*Takes a bundle of small pages out of the pocket
of her mantle.*] There are the loose scraps he dictated
it to me from. I hid them on the chance of some
such emergency. And if dear Mr. Tesman and I
were to put our heads together, I *do* think something
might come of it.

GEORGE.

Fancy ! I will dedicate my life—or all I can spare
of it—to the task. I seem to feel I owe him some
slight amends, perhaps. No use crying over spilt
milk, eh, Mrs. Elvsted ? We'll sit down—just you
and I—in the back drawing-room, and see if you can't
inspire me as you did him, eh ?

MRS. ELVSTED.

Oh, goodness, yes ! I should like it—if it only might
be possible !

    [GEORGE *and* MRS. ELVSTED *go into the back .
      drawing-room and become absorbed in*

eager conversation; HEDDA *sits in a chair in the front room, and a little later* BRACK *crosses over to her*

HEDDA.

[*In a low tone.*] Oh, Judge, *what* a relief to know that everything—including Lövborg's pistol—went off so well! In the breast! Isn't there a veil of unintentional beauty in that? Such an act of voluntary courage, too!

BRACK.

[*Smiles.*] H'm!—perhaps, dear Mrs. Hedda——

HEDDA.

[*Enthusiastically.*] But *wasn't* it sweet of him! To have the courage to live his own life after his own fashion—to break away from the banquet of life—*so* early and *so* drunk! A beautiful act like that *does* appeal to a superior woman's imagination!

BRACK.

Sorry to shatter your poetical illusions, little Mrs. Hedda, but, as a matter of fact, our lamented friend met his end under other circumstances. The shot did *not* strike him in the *breast*—but——   [*Pauses.*

HEDDA.

[*Excitedly.*] General Gabler's pistols! I might have known it! Did they *ever* shoot straight? Where *was* he hit, then?

BRACK.

[*In a discreet undertone.*] A little lower down!

HEDDA.

Oh, *how* disgusting!—how vulgar!—how ridiculous! —like everything else about me!

BRACK.

Yes, we're realistic types of human nature, and all that—but a trifle squalid, perhaps. And why did you give Lövborg your pistol, when it was certain to be traced by the police? ·For a charming cold-blooded woman with a clear head and no scruples, wasn't it just a leetle foolish!

HEDDA.

Perhaps; but I wanted him to do it beautifully, and he didn't! Oh, I've just admitted that I *did* give him the pistol—how annoyingly unwise of me! Now I'm in *your* power, I suppose?

BRACK.

Precisely—for some reason it's not easy to understand. But it's inevitable, and you know how you dread anything approaching scandal. All your past proceedings show that. [*To* GEORGE *and* MRS. ELVSTED *who come in together from the back-room.*] Well, how are you getting on with the reconstruction of poor Lövborg's great work, eh?

GEORGE.

Capitally; we've made out the first two parts already. And really, Hedda, I do believe Mrs. Elvsted *is* inspiring me; I begin to feel it coming on. Fancy that!

MRS. ELVSTED.

Yes, goodness ! Hedda, *won't* it be lovely if I can.
I mean to try *so* hard !

HEDDA.

Do, you dear little silly rabbit; and while you are
trying I will go into the back drawing-room and lie
down.

> [*She goes into the back room and draws the
> curtains. Short pause. Suddenly she is
> heard playing* "The Bogie Man" *within
> on the piano.*

GEORGE.

But, dearest Hedda, don't play "*The Bogie Man*"
this evening. As one of my aunts is dead, and poor
old Lövborg has shot himself, it seems just a little
pointed, eh?

HEDDA.

[*Puts her head out between the curtains.*] All right.

" What ! the accounts of all those everlasting bores settled ? '

I'll be quiet after this. I'm going to practise with the late General Gabler's pistol!

> [*Closes the curtains again;* GEORGE *gets behind the stove,* JUDGE BRACK *under the table, and* MRS. ELVSTED *under the sofa. A shot is heard within.*

GEORGE.

[*Behind the stove.*] Eh, look here, I tell you what — she's hit *me !* Think of that!

> [*His legs are visibly agitated for a short time. Another shot is heard.*

MRS. ELVSTED.

[*Under the sofa.*] Oh, please, not me! Oh, goodness, now I can't inspire anybody any more. Oh!

> [*Her feet, which can be seen under the valance, quiver a little and then are suddenly still.*

BRACK.

[*Vivaciously, from under the table.*] I say, Mrs. Hedda, I'm coming in every evening—we will have

great fun here togeth—— [*Another shot is heard.*]
Bless me! to bring down the poor old cock-of-the-walk—it's unsportsmanlike!—people don't *do* such things as that!

> [*The table-cloth is violently agitated for a
> minute, and presently the curtains open,
> and* HEDDA *appears.*

HEDDA.

[*Clearly and firmly.*] I've been trying in there to shoot myself beautifully—but with General Gabler's pistol—[*She lifts the tablecloth, then looks behind the stove and under the sofa.*] What! the accounts of all those everlasting bores settled? Then my suicide becomes unnecessary. Yes, I feel the courage of life once more!

> [*She goes into the back-room and plays* "The
> Funeral March of a Marionette" *as the
> Curtain falls.*]

THE WILD DUCK

THE WILD DUCK

ACT FIRST

At WERLE'S *house. In front a richly-upholstered study.
(R.) A green baize door leading to* WERLE'S *office.
At back, open folding doors, revealing an elegant
dining-room, in which a brilliant Norwegian
dinner-party is going on. Hired Waiters in pro-
fusion. A glass is tapped with a knife. Shouts
of "Bravo!" Old* Mr. WERLE *is heard making
a long speech, proposing—according to the custom
of Norwegian society on such occasions—the health
of his Housekeeper,* Mrs. SÖRBY. *Presently
several short-sighted, flabby, and thin-haired*

.

CHAMBERLAINS *enter from the dining-room with* HIALMAR EKDAL, *who writhes shyly under their remarks.*

A CHAMBERLAIN.

As we are the sole surviving specimens of Norwegian nobility, suppose we sustain our reputation as aristocratic sparklers by enlarging upon the enormous amount we have eaten, and chaffing Hialmar Ekdal, the friend of our host's son, for being a professional photographer?

THE OTHER CHAMBERLAINS.

Bravo! We will.

> [*They do; delight of* HIALMAR. Old WERLE
> *comes in, leaning on his Housekeeper's
> arm, followed by his son,* GREGERS
> WERLE.

OLD WERLE.

[*Dejectedly.*] Thirteen at table! [*To* GREGERS, *with a meaning glance at* HIALMAR.] This is the result of inviting an old college friend who has turned photographer! Wasting vintage wines on *him*, indeed. [*He passes on gloomily*.

HIALMAR.

[*To* GREGERS.] I am almost sorry I came. Your old min is *not* friendly. Yet he set me up as a photographer fifteen years ago. *Now* he takes me down! But for him, I should never have married Gina, who, you may remember, was a servant in your family once.

GREGERS.

What? my old college friend married fifteen years ago—and to our Gina, of all people! If I had not been up at the works all these years, I suppose I should have heard something of such an event. But my father never mentioned it. Odd!

[*He ponders;* OLD EKDAL *comes out through the green baize-door, bowing, and begging pardon, carrying copying work.* OLD

WERLE says " Ugh " and " Pah " in-
voluntarily.   HIALMAR shrinks back, and
looks another way.   A CHAMBERLAIN asks
him pleasantly if he knows that old man.

HIALMAR.

I—oh no.   Not in the least.   No relation !

GREGERS.

[*Shocked.*]   What, Hialmar, you, with your great
soul, deny your own father !

HIALMAR.

[*Vehemently.*]   Of course—what else *can* a photographer do with a disreputable old parent, who has
been in a penitentiary for making a fraudulent map ?
I shall leave this splendid banquet.   The Chamberlains are not kind to me, and I feel the crushing
hand of fate on my head !

[*Goes out hastily, feeling it.*

"Father, a word with you in private:
I loathe you."

Mrs. Sörby.

[*Archly.*] Any nobleman here say " Cold Punch " ?
[*Every nobleman says " Cold Punch " and
follows her out in search of it with enthusiasm.* Gregers *approaches his father,
who wishes he would go.*

Gregers.

Father, a word with you in private. I loathe you.
I am nothing if not candid. Old Ekdal was your
partner once, and it's my firm belief you deserved a
prison quite as much as he did. However, you surely
need not have married our Gina to my old friend
Hialmar. You know very well she was no better than
she should have been !

Old Werle.

True—but then no more is Mrs. Sörby. And *I*
am going to marry *her*—if you have no objection,
that is.

GREGERS.

None in the world!   How can I object to a step-
mother who is playing Blind Man's Buff at the
present moment with the Norwegian nobility?   I am
not so overstrained as all that.   But really I can*not*
allow my old friend Hialmar, with his great, con-
fiding, childlike mind, to remain in contented ignorance of Gina's past.   No, I see my mission in life at
last!   I shall take my hat, and inform him that his
home is built upon a lie.   He will be *so* much
obliged to me !   · [*Takes his hat, and goes out.*

OLD WERLE.

Ha !—I am a wealthy merchant, of dubious morals,
and I am about to marry my housekeeper, who is on
intimate terms with the Norwegian aristocracy.   I
have a son who loathes me, and who is either an
Ibsenian satire on the Master's own ideals, or else an
utterly impossible prig—I don't know or care which.
Altogether, I flatter myself my household affords an
accurate and realistic picture of Scandinavian Society !

Curtain.

ACT SECOND

HIALMAR EKDAL'S *Photographic Studio. Cameras, neck-rests, and other instruments of torture lying about.* GINA EKDAL *and* HEDWIG, *her daughter, aged* 14, *and wearing spectacles, discovered sitting up for* HIALMAR.

HEDVIG.

Grandpapa is in his room with a bottle of brandy and a jug of hot water, doing some fresh copying work. Father is in society, dining out. He promised he would bring me home something nice!

HIALMAR.

[*Coming in, in evening dress.*] And he has not forgotten his promise, my child. Behold! [*He *presents her with the menu card;* HEDVIG *gulps down her tears;* HIALMAR *notices her disappointment, with annoyance.*] And this all the gratitude I get! After dining out and coming home in a dress-coat and boots, which are disgracefully tight! Well well, just to show you how hurt I am, I won't have any *beer* now! What a selfish brute I am! [*Relenting.*] You may bring me just a little drop. [*He bursts into tears.*] I will play you a plaintive Bohemian dance on my flute. [*He does.*] No beer at such a sacred moment as this! [*He drinks.*] Ha, this is real domestic bliss!

[GREGERS WERLE *comes in, in a countrified suit.*

GREGERS.

I have left my father's home—dinner-party and all —for ever. I am coming to lodge with you.

HIALMAR.

[*Still melancholy.*] Have some bread and butter. You won't?—then I *will.* I want it, after your father's lavish hospitality. [HEDVIG *goes to fetch bread and butter.*] My daughter—a poor short-sighted little thing—but mine own.

GREGERS.

My father has had to take to strong glasses, too—he can hardly see after dinner. [*To* Old EKDAL, *who stumbles in very drunk.*] How can you, Lieutenant Ekdal, who were such a keen sportsman once, live in this poky little hole?

OLD EKDAL.

I am a sportsman still. The only difference is that once I shot bears in a forest, and now I pot tame rabbits in a garret. Quite as amusing—and safer. [*He goes to sleep on a sofa.*

HIALMAR.

[*With pride.*] It is quite true. You shall see.

[*He pushes back sliding doors, and reveals a garret full of rabbits and poultry— moonlight effect.* HEDVIG *returns with bread and butter.*

HEDVIG.

[*To* GREGERS.] If you stand just there, you get the best view of our Wild Duck. We are very proud of her, because she gives the play its title, you know, and has to be brought into the dialogue a good deal. Your father peppered her out shooting, and we saved her life.

HIALMAR.

Yes, Gregers, our estate is not large—but still we preserve, you see. And my poor old father and I sometimes get a day's gunning in the garret. He shoots with a pistol, which my illiterate wife here *will* call a " pigstol." He once, when he got into trouble, pointed it at himself. But the descendant of two lieutenant-colonels who had never quailed before living rabbit yet, faltered then. He *didn't* shoot. Then I put it to my own head. But at the decisive moment, I won the victory over myself. I remained in life. Now we only shoot rabbits and fowls with it. After all I am very happy and contented as I am.   [*He eats some bread and butter.*

GREGERS.

But you ought *not* to be. You have a good deal of the Wild Duck about you. So have your wife and daughter. You are living in marsh vapours. To-morrow I will take you out for a walk and explain what I mean. It is my mission in life. Good night!

[*He goes out.*

GINA AND HEDWIG.

What *was* the gentleman talking about, father?

HIALMAR.

[*Eating bread and butter.*] He has been dining, you know. No matter—what *we* have to do now, is to put my disreputable old whitehaired pariah of a parent to bed.

[*He and* GINA *lift* Old ECCLES—*we mean* Old EKDAL—*up by the legs and arms, and take him off to bed as the Curtain falls.*

ACT THREE

HIALMAR's *Studio. A photograph has just been taken.*
GINA *and* HEDVIG *are tidying up.*

GINA.

[*Apologetically.*] There *should* have been a luncheon-
party in this act, with Dr. Relling and Mölvik, who
would have been in a state of comic " chippiness,"
after his excesses overnight. But, as it hadn't much
to do with such plot as there is, we cut it out. It
came cheaper. Here comes your father back from
his walk with that lunatic, young Werle—you had
better go and play with the Wild Duck.

[HEDVIG *goes.*

HIALMAR.

[*Coming in.*] I have been for a walk with Gregers; he meant well—but it was tiring. Gina, he has told me that, fifteen years ago, before I married you, you were rather a Wild Duck, so to speak. [*Severely.*] Why haven't you been writhing in penitence and remorse all these years, eh?

GINA.

[*Sensibly.*] Why? Because I have had other things to do. *You* wouldn't take any photographs, so I *had* to.

HIALMAR.

All the same—it was a swamp of deceit. And where am I to find elasticity of spirit to bring out my grand invention now? I used to shut myself up in the parlour, and ponder and cry, when I thought that the effort of inventing anything would sap my vitality. [*Pathetically.*] I *did* want to leave you an inventor's widow; but I never shall now, particularly

as I haven't made up my mind what to invent yet.
Yes, it's all over. Rabbits are trash, and even
poultry palls. And I'll wring that cursed Wild
Duck's neck !

GREGERS.

[*Coming in beaming.*] Well, so you've got it over.
Wasn't it soothing and ennobling, eh ? and *ain't* you
both obliged to me ?

GINA.

No; it's my opinion you'd better have minded
your own business.   [*Weeps.*

GREGERS.

[*In great surprise.*] Bless me ! Pardon my Norwegian *naïveté,* but this ought really to be quite a
new starting-point. Why, I confidently expected to
have found you both beaming !—Mrs. Ekdal, being
so illiterate, may take some little time to see it—but
you, Hialmar, with your deep mind, surely *you* feel
a new consecration, eh ?

HIALMAR.

[*Dubiously.*] Oh—er—yes. I suppose so—in a sort of way.   [HEDVIG *runs in, overjoyed.*

HEDVIG.

Father, only see what Mrs. Sörby has given me for a birthday present—a beautiful deed of gift !

[*Shows it.*

HIALMAR.

[*Eluding her.*] Ha! Mrs. Sörby, the family house-keeper. My father's sight failing ! Hedvig in goggles ! What vistas of heredity these astonishing coincidences open up ! *I* am not short-sighted, at all events, and I see it all—all ! *This* is my answer. [*He takes the deed, and tears it across.*] Now I have nothing more to do in this house. [*Puts on over-coat.*] My home has fallen in ruins about me. [*Bursts into tears.*] My hat !

GREGERS.

Oh, but you *mustn't* go. You must be all three

together, to attain the true frame of mind for self-sacrificing forgiveness, you know!

HIALMAR.

Self-sacrificing forgiveness be blowed!

> [*He tears himself away, and goes out.*

HEDVIG.

[*With despairing eyes.*] Oh, he said it might be blowed! Now he'll *never* come home any more!

GREGERS.

Shall I tell you how to regain your father's confidence, and bring him home surely? Sacrifice the Wild Duck.

HEDVIG.

Do you think that will do any good?

GREGERS.

You just *try* it!

Curtain.

ACT FOURTH

Same Scene. GREGERS *enters, and finds* GINA *retouching photographs.*

GREGERS.

[*Pleasantly.*] Hialmar not come in yet, after last night, I suppose?

GINA.

Not he! He's been out on the loose all night with Relling and Mölvik. Now he's snoring on their sofa.

GREGERS.

[*Disappointed.*] Dear!—dear!—when he ought to be yearning to wrestle in solitude and self-examination!

GINA.

[*Rudely.*] Self-examine your grandmother!

[*She goes out;* HEDVIG *comes in.*

GREGERS.

[*To* HEDVIG.] Ah, I see you haven't found courage to settle the Wild Duck yet!

HEDVIG.

No—it seemed such a delightful idea at first.   Now it strikes me as a trifle—well, *Ibsenish.*

GREGERS.

[*Reprovingly.*] I *thought* you hadn't grown up quite unharmed in this house!   But if you really had the true, joyous spirit of self-sacrifice, you'd have a shot at that Wild Duck, if you died for it!

HEDVIG.

[*Slowly.*] I see; you mean that my constitution's changing, and I ought to behave as such?

GREGERS.

Exactly, I'm what Americans would term a " crank "
—but *I* believe in you, Hedvig.

> [HEDVIG *takes down the pistol from the
> mantelpiece, and goes into the garret with
> flashing eyes;* GINA *comes in.*

HIALMAR.

[*Looking in at door with hesitation; he is unwashed
and dishevelled.*] Has anybody happened to see my
hat ?

GINA.

Gracious, what a sight you are ! Sit done and have
some breakfast, do.   [*She brings it.*

HIALMAR.

[*Indignantly.*] What! touch food under *this* roof ?
Never ! [*Helps himself to bread-and-butter and coffee.*]
Go and pack up my scientific uncut books, my manu-
scripts, and all the best rabbits, in my portmanteau.
I am going away for ever. On second thoughts, I

shall stay in the spare room for another day or two—
it won't be the same as living with you!

> [*He takes some salt meat.*

GREGERS.

Must you go? Just when you've got nice firm
ground to build upon—thanks to me! Then there's
your great invention, too.

HIALMAR.

Everything's invented already. And I only cared
about my invention because, although it doesn't exist
yet, I thought Hedvig believed in it, with all the
strength of her sweet little shortsighted eyes! But
now I don't believe in Hedvig!

> [*He pours himself out another cup of coffee.*

GREGERS.

[*Earnestly.*] But, Hialmar, if I can prove to you
that she is ready to sacrifice her cherished Wild
Duck? See!

> [*He pushes back sliding-door, and discovers*
> HEDVIG *aiming at the* Wild Duck *with the*
> *butt-end of the pistol. Tableau.*

GINA.

[*Excitedly.*] But don't you *see?* It's the pigstol—
that fatal Norwegian weapon which, in Ibsenian
dramas, *never* shoots straight! And she has got it by
the wrong end too. She will shoot herself!

GREGERS.

[*Quietly.*] She will! Let the child make amends.
It will be a most realistic and impressive finale!

GINA.

No, no—put down the pigstol, Hedvig. Do you
hear, child?

HEDVIG.

[*Still aiming.*] I hear—but I shan't unless father
tells me to.

GREGERS.

Hialmar, show the great soul I always *said* you had.
This sorrow will set free what is noble in you. Don't
spoil a fine situation. Be a man! Let the child
shoot herself!

HIALMAR.

[*Irresolutely.*] Well, really, I don't know.   There's a good deal in what Gregers says.   II'm!

GINA.

A good deal of tomfool rubbish!   I'm illiterate, I know.   I've been a Wild Duck in my time, and I waddle.   But for all that, I'm the only person in the play with a grain of common-sense.   And I'm sure— whatever Mr. Ibsen or Gregers choose to say—that a screaming burlesque like this ought *not* to end like a tragedy—even in this queer Norway of ours!   And it shan't, either!   Tell the child to put that nasty pigstol down, and come away—do!

HIALMAR.

[*Yielding.*] Ah, well, I am a farcical character myself, after all.   Don't touch a hair of that duck's head, Hedvig.   Come to my arms and all shall be forgiven!

> [HEDVIG *throws down the pistol—which goes*
> *off and kills a rabbit—and rushes into her*

"Put that nasty pigstol down!"

father's arms. Old EKDAL *comes out of a corner with a fowl on each shoulder, and bursts into tears. Affecting family picture.*

GREGERS.

[*Annoyed.*] It's all very pretty, I dare say—but it's not Ibsen! My real mission is to be the thirteenth at table. I don't know what I mean—but I fly to fulfil it! [*He goes.*

HIALMAR.

And now we've got rid of *him*, Hedvig, fetch me the deed of gift I tore up, and a slip of paper, and a penny bottle of gum, and we'll soon make a valid instrument of it again.

[*He pastes the torn deed together as the Curtain slowly descends.*

PILL-DOCTOR HERDAL

PILL-DOCTOR HERDAL

[PREFATORY NOTE.—The original title—*Mester-Pjil-drögster Herdal*—would sound a trifle too uncouth to the Philistine ear, and is therefore modified as above, although the term "drögster," strictly speaking, denotes a practitioner who has not received a regular diploma].

ACT FIRST

An elegantly furnished drawing-room at Dr. HERDAL'S. In front, on the left, a console-table, on which is a large round bottle full of coloured water. On the right a stove, with a banner-screen made out of a richly-embroidered chest-protector. On the stove, a stethoscope and a small galvanic battery. In one corner, a hat and umbrella stand : in another, a

desk, at which stands SENNA BLAKDRAF, *making
out the quarterly accounts. Through a glass-door
at the back is seen the Dispensary, where* RÜBUB
KALOMEL *is seated, occupied in rolling a pill.
Both go on working in perfect silence for four
minutes and a half.*

DR. HAUSTUS HERDAL.

[*Enters through hall-door ; he is elderly, with a
plain sensible countenance, but slightly weak hair and
expression.*] Come here Miss Blakdraf. [*Hangs up
hat, and throws his mackintosh on a divan.*] Have
you made out all those bills yet?

[*Looks sternly at her.*

SENNA.

[*In a low hesitating voice.*] Almost. I have
charged each patient with three attendances daily.
Even when you only dropped in for a cup of tea and
a chat. [*Passionately.*] I felt I *must*—I *must !*

Dr. Herdal.

[*Alters his tone, clasps her head in his hands, and whispers.*] I wish you could make out the bills for me, *always.*

Senna.

[*In nervous exaltation.*] How lovely that would be! Oh, you are so unspeakably good to me! It is too enthralling to be here!

[*Sinks down and embraces his knees.*

Dr. Herdal.

So I've understood. [*With suppressed irritation.*] For goodness' sake, let go my legs! I do *wish* you wouldn't be so confoundedly neurotic!

Rübub.

[*Has risen, and comes in through glass-door, breathing with difficulty; he is a prematurely bald young man of fifty-five, with a harelip, and squints slightly.*] I beg pardon, Dr. Herdal, I see I interrupt

you. [*As* Senna *rises.*] I have just completed this
pill.   Have you looked at it ?

> [*He offers it for inspection, diffidently.*

Dr. Herdal.

[*Evasively.*] It appears to be a pill of the usual
dimensions.

Rübub.

[*Cast down.*] All these years you have never given
me one encouraging word ! *Can't* you praise my
pill ?

Dr. Herdal.

[*Struggles with himself.*] I—I cannot.   You should
not attempt to compound pills on your own account.

Rübub.

[*Breathing laboriously.*] And yet there was a time
when *you*, too——

Dr. Herdal.

[*Complacently.*] Yes, it was certainly a pill that
came as a lucky stepping-stone—but not a pill like
that !

" For goodness' sake, let go my legs ! "

L

RÜBUB.

[*Vehemently.*] Listen! Is that your last word? *Is* my aged mother to pass out of this world without ever knowing whether I am competent to construct an effective pill or not?

DR. HERDAL.

[*As if in desperation.*] You had better try it upon your mother—it will enable her to form an opinion. Only mind—I will not be responsible for the result.

RÜBUB.

I understand. Exactly as you tried *your* pill, all those years ago, upon Dr. Ryval.

[*He bows and goes out.*

DR. HERDAL.

[*Uneasily.*] He said that so strangely, Senna. But tell me now—when are you going to marry him?

SENNA.

[*Starts—half glancing up at him.*] I—I don't know. This year—next year—now—*never!* I cannot marry him . . . I cannot—I *cannot*—it is so utterly impossible to leave you!

DR. HERDAL.

Yes, I can understand *that*. But, my poor Senna, hadn't you better take a little walk?

SENNA.

[*Clasps her hands gratefully.*] How sweet and thoughtful you are to me! I *will* take a walk.

DR. HERDAL.

[*With a suppressed smile.*] Do! And—h'm!—you needn't trouble to come back. I have advertised for a male book-keeper—they are less emotional. Good-night, my little Senna!

SENNA.

[*Softly and quiveringly.*] Good-night, Dr. Herdal!

[*Staggers out of hall-door, blowing kisses.*

MRS. HERDAL.

[*Enters through the window, plaintively.*] Quite an acquisition for you, Haustus, this Miss Blakdraf!

DR. HERDAL.

She's—h'm—extremely civil and obliging. But I am parting with her, Aline—mainly on *your* account.

MRS. HERDAL.

[*Evades him.*] Was it on my account, indeed, Haustus? You have parted with so many young persons on my account—so you tell me!

DR. HERDAL.

[*Depressed.*] Oh, but this is hopeless! When I have tried so hard to bring a ray of sunlight into your desolate life! I must give Rübub Kalomel notice too—his pill is really too preposterous!

Mrs. Herdal.

[*Feels gropingly for a chair, and sits down on the floor.*] Him, *too !* Ah, Haustus, you will never make my home a real home for me. My poor first husband, Halvard Solness, tried—and *he* couldn't ! When one has had such misfortunes as I have—all the family portraits burnt, and the silk dresses, too, and a pair of twins, and nine lovely dolls.

[*Chokes with tears.*

Dr. Herdal.

[*As if to lead her away from the subject.*] Yes, yes, yes, that must have been a heavy blow for you, my poor Aline. I can understand that your spirits can never be really high again. And then for poor Master Builder Solness to be so taken up with that Miss Wangel as he was—that, too, was so wretched for you. To see him topple off the tower, as he did that day ten years ago——

Mrs. Herdal.

Yes, that too, Haustus. But I did not mind it so much—it all seemed so perfectly natural in both of them.

Dr. Herdal.

Natural! For a girl of twenty three to taunt a middle-aged architect, whom she knew to be constitutionally liable to giddiness, never to let him have any peace till he had climbed a spire as dizzy as himself—and all for the fun of seeing him fall off— how in the world——!

Mrs. Herdal.

[*Laying the table for supper with dried fish and punch.*] The younger generation have a keener sense of humour than we elder ones, Haustus, and perhaps after all, she was only a perplexing sort of allegory.

Dr. Herdal.

Yes, that would explain her to some extent, no doubt. But how *he* could be such an old fool!

Mrs. Herdal.

That Miss Wangel was a strangely fascinating type of girl. Why, even I myself——

Dr. Herdal.

[*Sits down and takes some fish.*] Fascinating? Well, goodness knows, I couldn't see *that* at all. [*Seriously.*] Has it never struck you, Aline, that elderly Norwegians are so deucedly impressionable— mere bundles of overstrained nerves, hypersensitive ganglia. Except, of course, the Medical Profession.

Mrs. Herdal.

Yes, of course; those in that profession are not so inclined to gangle. And when one has succeeded by such a stroke of luck as you have——

Dr. Herdal.

[*Drinks a glass of punch.*] You're right enough there. If I had not been called in to prescribe for Dr. Ryval, who used to have the leading practice here, I should never have stepped so wonderfully into his shoes as I did. [*Changes to a tone of quiet chuckling merriment.*] Let me tell you a funny story, Aline; it sounds a ludicrous thing—but all my good fortune here was based upon a simple little pill. For if Dr. Ryval had never taken it——

Mrs. Herdal.

[*Anxiously.*] Then you *do* think it was the pill that caused him to——?

Dr. Herdal.

On the contrary; I am perfectly sure the pill had nothing whatever to do with it—the inquest made it quite clear that it was really the liniment. But don't you see, Aline, what tortures me night and day is the thought that it *might* unconsciously have been the pill which—— Never to be free from *that !* To have such a thought gnawing and burning always—always, like a moral mustard plaster !

[*He takes more punch.*

Mrs. Herdal.

Yes; I suppose there is a poultice of that sort burning on every breast—and we must never take it off either—it is our simple duty to keep it on. I too, Haustus, am haunted by a fancy that if this Miss Wangel were to ring at our bell now——

Dr. Herdal.

After she has been lost sight of for ten years? She is safe enough in some sanatorium, depend upon it. And what if she *did* come? Do you think, my dear good woman, that I—a sensible clear-headed general practitioner, who have found out all I know for myself—would let her play the deuce with me as she did with poor Halvard? No, general practitioners don't *do* such things—even in Norway!

Mrs. Herdal.

Don't they indeed, Haustus? [*The surgery-bell rings loudly.*] Did you hear *that?* There she is! I will go and put on my best cap. It is my duty to show her *that* small attention.

DR. HERDAL.

[*Laughing nervously.*] Why, what on earth !——
It's the night-bell. It is most probably the new
book-keeper ! [MRS. HERDAL *goes out ;* DR. HERDAL
rises with difficulty, and opens the door.] Goodness
gracious !—it *is* that girl, after all !

[HILDA WANGEL *enters through the dispensary door.
She wears a divided skirt, thick boots, and a Tam
o' Shanter with an eagle's wing in it. Somewhat
freckled. Carries a green tin cylinder slung round her,
and a rug in a strap. Goes straight up to* HERDAL,
her eyes sparkling with happiness.] How are you ?
I've run you down, you see ! The ten years are up.
Isn't it scrumptiously thrilling, to see me like this ?

DR. HERDAL.

[*Politely retreating.*] It is—very much so—but still
I don't in the least understand——

HILDA.

[*Measures him with a glance.*] Oh, you *will*. I
have come to be of use to you. I've no luggage, and
no money. Not that *that* makes any difference. I
never *have*. And I've been allured and attracted
here. You surely know how these things come
about?   [*Throws her arms round him.*

DR. HERDAL.

What the deuce! Miss Wangel, you *mustn't*. I'm
a married man! There's my wife!

MRS. HERDAL *enters*.

HILDA.

As if *that* mattered—it's only dear, sweet Mrs.
Solness. *She* doesn't mind—*do* you, dear Mrs. Solness?

MRS. HERDAL.

It does not seem to be of much *use* minding, Miss
Wangel. I presume you have come to stay?

HILDA.

[*In amused surprise.*] Why, of course—what else should I come for ? I *always* come to stay, until— h'm !   [*Nods slowly, and sits down at table.*

DR. HERDAL.

[*Involuntarily.*] She's drinking my punch ! If she thinks I'm going to stand this sort of thing, she's mistaken. I'll soon show her a pill-doctor is a very different kind of person from a mere Master Builder !

> [HILDA *finishes the punch with an indefin-*
> *able expression in her eyes, and* DR.
> HERDAL *looks on gloomily as the Curtain*
> *falls.*

ACT SECOND

DR. HERDAL'S *drawing-room and dispensary, as before. It is early in the day.* DR. HERDAL *sits by the little table, taking his own temperature with a clinical thermometer. By the door stands the* NEW BOOK-KEEPER; *he wears blue spectacles and a discoloured white tie, and seems slightly nervous.*

DR. HERDAL.

Well, now you understand what is necessary. My late book-keeper, Miss Blakdraf, used to keep my accounts very cleverly—she charged every visit twice over.

The New Book-keeper.

I am familiar with book-keeping by double entry. I was once employed at a bank.

Dr. Herdal.

I am discharging my assistant, too; he was always trying to push me out with his pills. Perhaps you will be able to dispense?

The New Book-keeper.

[*Modestly.*] With an additional salary, I should be able to do that too.

Dr. Herdal.

Capital! You *shall* dispense with an additional salary. Go into the dispensary, and see what you can make of it. You may mistake a few drugs at first —but everything must have a beginning.

> [*As the* New Book-keeper *retires,* Mrs. Herdal *enters in a hat and cloak with a watering-pot, noiselessly.*

Mrs. Herdal.

Miss Wangel got up early, before breakfast, and went for a walk.   She is so wonderfully vivacious!

Dr. Herdal.

So I should say.   But tell me, Aline, is she *really* going to stay with us here?   [*Nervously.*

Mrs. Herdal.

[*Looks at him.*] So she tells me.   And, as she has brought nothing with her except a tooth-brush and a powder-puff, I am going into the town to get her a few articles.   We *must* make her feel at home.

Dr. Herdal.

[*Breaking out.*] I *will* make her not only *feel* but *be* at home, wherever that is, this very day!   I will *not* have a perambulating Allegory without a portmanteau here on an indefinite visit.   I say, she shall go—do you hear, Aline?   Miss Wangel will go!

[*Raps with his fist on table.*

Mrs. Herdal.

[*Quietly.*] If you say so, Haustus, no doubt she will *have* to go. But you must tell her so yourself.

> [*Puts the watering-pot on the console table,
> and goes out, as* Hilda *enters, sparkling
> with pleasure.*

Hilda.

[*Goes up straight to him.*] Good morning, Dr. Herdal. I have just seen a pig killed. It was *ripping*—I mean, gloriously thrilling! And your wife has taken a tremendous fancy to me. Fancy *that!*

Dr. Herdal.

[*Gloomily.*] It *is* eccentric certainly. But my poor dear wife was always a little——

Hilda.

[*Nods her head slowly several times.*] So *you* have noticed that too? I have had a long talk with her. She can't get over your discharging Mr. Kalomel—he is the only man who ever *really* understood her.

M

Dr. Herdal.

If I could only pay her off a little bit of the huge, immeasurable debt I owe her—but I *ran't*!

Hilda.

[*Looks hard at him.*] Can't *I* help you? I helped Ragnar Brovik. Didn't you know I stayed with him and poor little Kaia—after that accident to my Master Builder? I did. I made Ragnar build me the loveliest castle in the air—lovelier, even, than poor Mr. Solness's would have been—and we stood together on the very top. The steps were rather too much for Kaia. Besides, there was no room for her on top. And he put towering spires on all his semi-detached villas. Only, somehow, they didn't let. Then the castle in the air tumbled down, and Ragnar went into liquidation, and I continued my walking-tour.

Dr. Herdal.

[*Interested against his will.*] And where did you go after *that*, may I ask, Miss Wangel?

HILDA.

Oh, ever so far north. There I met Mr. and Mrs.
Tesman—the second Mrs. Tesman—she who was Mrs.
Elvsted, with the irritating hair, you know. They
were on their honeymoon, and had just decided that
it was impossible to reconstruct poor Mr. Lövborg's
great book out of Mrs. Elvsted's rough notes. But I
insisted on George's attempting the impossible—with
Me. And what *do* you think Mrs. Tesman wears in
her hair *now ?*

DR. HERDAL.

Why, really I could not say. Vine-leaves, perhaps.

HILDA.

Wrong—*straws !* Poor Tesman *didn't* fancy that—
so he shot himself, *un*-beautifully, through his ticket-
pocket. And I went on and took Rosmersholm for
the summer. There had been misfortune in the
house, so it was to let. Dear good old Rector Kroll
acted as my reference; his wife and children had no

sympathy with his views, so I used to see him every day. And I persuaded him, too, to attempt the impossible—he had never ridden anything but a rocking-horse in his life, but I made him promise to mount the White Horse of Rosmershölm. He didn't get over *that.* They found his body, a fortnight afterwards, in the mill-dam.   Thrilling !

DR. HERDAL.

[*Shakes his finger at her.*] What a girl you are, Miss Wangel ! But you mustn't play these games *here*, you know.

HILDA.

[*Laughs to herself.*] Of course not.   But I suppose I *am* a strange sort of bird.

DR. HERDAL.

You are like a strong tonic.   When I look at you I seem to be regarding an effervescing saline draught. Still, I really must decline to take you.

HILDA.

[*A little sulky.*] That is not how you spoke ten years ago, up at the mountain station, when you were such a flirt!

DR. HERDAL.

Was I a flirt? Deuce take me if I remember. But I am not like that *now*.

HILDA.

Then you have really forgotten how you sat next to me at the *table d'hôte*, and made pills and swallowed them, and were so splendid and buoyant and free that all the old women who knitted left next day?

DR. HERDAL.

What a memory you have for trifles, Miss Wangel; it's quite wonderful!

HILDA.

Trifles! There was no trifling on *your* part. When you promised to come back in ten years, like a troll, and fetch me!

DR. HERDAL.

Did I say all that? It *must* have been *after table d'hôte!*

HILDA.

It was. I was a mere chit then—only twenty-three; but *I* remember. And now *I* have come for *you.*

DR. HERDAL.

Dear, dear! But there is nothing of the troll about me now I have married Mrs. Solness.

HILDA.

[*Looking sharply at him.*] Yes, I remember you were always dropping in to tea in those days.

DR. HERDAL.

[*Seems hurt.*] Every visit was duly put down in the ledger and charged for—as poor little Senna will tell you.

HILDA.

Little Senna? Oh, Dr. Herdal, I believe there is a bit of the troll left in you still!

DR. HERDAL.

[*Laughs a little.*] No, no; my conscience is perfectly robust—always was.

HILDA.

Are you quite *quite* sure that, when you went indoors with dear Mrs. Solness that afternoon, and left me alone with my Master Builder, you did not foresee—perhaps wish—intend, even a little, that—— H'm?

DR. HERDAL.

That you would talk the poor man into clambering up that tower? You want to drag *Me* into that business now!

HILDA.

[*Teasingly.*] Yes, I certainly think that then you went on exactly like a troll.

DR. HERDAL.

[*With uncontrollable emotion.*] Hilda, there is not a corner of me safe from you! Yes, I see now that *must* have been the way of it. Then I *was* a troll in that, too! But isn't it terrible the price I have had to pay for it? To have a wife who—— No, I shall never roll a pill again—never, never!

HILDA.

[*Lays her head on the stove, and answers as if half asleep.*] No more pills? Poor Doctor Herdal!

DR. HERDAL.

[*Bitterly.*] No—nothing but cosy commonplace grey powders for a whole troop of children.

HILDA.

[*Lively again.*] Not *grey* powders! [*Quite seriously.*] I will tell you what you shall make next. Beautiful

" Beautiful rainbow-coloured powders that will give
one a real grip on the world ! "

rainbow-coloured powders that will give one a real grip on the world. Powders to make every one free and buoyant, and ready to grasp at one's own happiness, to *dare* what one *would*. I will have you make them. I will—I *will!*

Dr. Herdal.

H'm! I am not quite sure that I clearly understand. And then the ingredients—— ?

Hilda.

What stupid people all of you pill-doctors are, to be sure! Why, they will be *poisons*, of course!

Dr. Herdal.

Poisons? Why in the world should they be *that?*

Hilda.

[*Without answering him.*] All the thrillingest, deadliest poisons—it is only such things that are wholesome, nowadays.

Dr. Herdal.

[*As if caught by her enthusiasm.*] And I could colour them, too, by exposing them to rays cast through a prism. Oh, Hilda, how I have needed you all these years! For, you see, with *her* it was impossible to discuss such things. [*Embraces her.*

Mrs. Herdal.

[*Enters noiselessly through hall-door.*] I suppose, Haustus, you are persuading Miss Wangel to start by the afternoon steamer? I have bought her a pair of curling-tongs, and a packet of hair-pins. The larger parcels are coming on presently.

Dr. Herdal.

[*Uneasily.*] H'm! Hilda—Miss Wangel I *should* say—is kindly going to stay on a little longer, to assist me in some scientific experiments. You wouldn't understand them if I told you.

Mrs. Herdal.

Shouldn't I, Haustus? I daresay not.

[*The* New Book-keeper *looks through the glass
door of dispensary.*

Hilda.

[*Starts violently and points—then in a whisper.*]
Who is *that?*

Dr. Herdal.

Only the new Book-keeper and Assistant—a very
intelligent person.

Hilda.

[*Looks straight in front of her with a far-away expression, and whispers to herself.*] I thought at first it
was . . . . But no—*that* would be *too* frightfully
thrilling!

Dr. Herdal.

[*To himself.*] I'm turning into a regular old troll

now—but I can't help myself.   After all, I am only an elderly Norwegian.   We are *made* like that . . . . Rainbow powders—*real* rainbow powders!   With Hilda! . . . . Oh, to have the joy of life once more!

[*Takes his temperature again as Curtain falls.*

ACT THIRD

[*On the right, a smart verandah, attached to* DR. HERDAL'S *dwelling-house, and communicating with the drawing-room and dispensary by glass doors. On the left a tumble-down rockery, with a headless plaster Mercury. In front, a lawn, with a large silvered glass globe on a stand. Chairs and tables. All the furniture is of galvanised iron. A sunset is seen going on among the trees.*

DR. HERDAL.

[*Comes out of dispensary-door cautiously, and whispers.*] Hilda, are you in there?

   [*Taps with fingers on drawing-room door.*

HILDA.

[*Comes out with a half-teasing smile.*] Well—and how is the rainbow-powder getting on, Dr. Herdal ?

DR. HERDAL.

[*With enthusiasm.*] It is getting on simply splendidly. I sent the new assistant out to take a little walk, so that he should not be in the way. There is arsenic in the powder, Hilda, and digitalis too, and strychnine, and the best beetle-killer !

HILDA.

[*With happy, wondering eyes.*] *Lots* of beetle-killer   And you will give some of it to *her*, to make her free and buoyant. I think one really *has* the right—when people happen to stand in the way—— !

DR. HERDAL.

Yes, you may well say so, Hilda. Still—[*dubiously*] —it *does* occur to me that such doings may perhaps be misunderstood—by the narrow-minded and conventional.   [*They go on the lawn, and sit down.*

HILDA.

[*With an outburst.*] Oh, that all seems to me so foolish—so irrelevant!· As if the whole thing wasn't intended as an allegory!

DR. HERDAL.

[*Relieved.*] Ah, so long as it is merely *allegorical,* of course—— But what is it an allegory *of*, Hilda?

HILDA.

[*Reflects in vain.*] How can you sit there and ask such questions? I suppose I am a symbol—of some sort.

DR. HERDAL.

[*As a thought flashes upon him.*] A cymbal? That would certainly account for your bra—— Then, am *I* a cymbal too, Hilda?

HILDA.

Why yes—what else? You represent the artist-worker, or the elder generation, or the pursuit of

N

the ideal, or a bilious conscience—or something or other. *You're* all right!

DR. HERDAL.

[*Shakes his head.*] Am I? But I don't quite see —— Well, well, cymbals are meant to clash a little. And I see plainly now that I ought to prescribe this powder for as many as possible. Isn't it terrible, Hilda, that so many poor souls never really die their own deaths—pass out of the world without even the formality of an inquest? As the district Coroner, I feel strongly on the subject.

HILDA.

And, when the Coroner has finished sitting on all the bodies, perhaps—but I shan't tell you now. [*Speaks as if to a child.*] There, run away and finish making the rainbow-powder, do!

DR. HERDAL.

[*Skips up into the dispensary.*] I will—I will! Oh, I do feel such a troll—such a light-haired, light-headed old devil!

RÜBUB.

[*Enters garden-gate.*] I have had my dismissal—but I'm not going without saying good-bye to Mrs. Herdal.

HILDA.

Dr. Herdal would disapprove—you really must not, Mr. Kalomel. And, besides, Mrs. Herdal is not at home. She is in the town buying me a reel of cotton. *Dr.* Herdal is in. He is making real rainbow powders for regenerating everybody all round. Won't *that* be fun ?

RÜBUB.

Making powders ? Ha ! ha ! But you will see he won't *take* one himself. It is quite notorious to us younger men that he simply daren't do it.

HILDA.

[*With a little snort of contempt.*] Oh, I daresay— that's so likely ! [*Defiantly.*] I know he *can*, though. I've *seen* him !

Rübub.

There is a tradition that he once—but not now
—he knows better. I think you said Mrs. Herdal
was in the town? I will go and look for her. I
understand her so well.   [*Goes out by gate.*

Hilda.

[*Calls.*] Dr. Herdal! Come out this minute. I
want you—awfully!

Dr. Herdal.

[*Puts his head out.*] Just when I am making such
wonderful progress with the powder. [*Comes down
and leans on a table.*] Have you hit upon some way
of giving it to Aline? I thought if you were to put
it in her arrowroot——?

Hilda.

No, thanks. I won't have that now. I have just
recollected that it is a rule of mine never to injure
anybody I have once been formally introduced to.

Strangers don't count. No, poor Mrs. Herdal mustn't take that powder !

DR. HERDAL.

[*Disappointed.*] Then is nothing to come of making rainbow powders, after all, Hilda ?

HILDA.

[*Looks hard at him.*] People say you are afraid to take your own physic. Is that true ?

DR. HERDAL.

Yes, I am. [*After a pause—with candour.*] I find it invariably disagrees with me.

HILDA.

[*With a half-dubious smile.*] I think I can understand *that*. But you did *once*. You swallowed your own pills that day at the *table d'hôte*, ten years ago. And I heard a harp in the air, too !

DR. HERDAL.

[*Open-mouthed.*] I don't think that *could* have been me. I don't play any instrument. And that was quite a special thing, too. It's not every day I can do it. Those were only *bread* pills, Hilda.

HILDA.

[*With flashing eyes.*] But you rolled them, you took them. And I want to see you stand once more free and high and great, swallowing your own pre-parations. [*Passionately.*] I *will* have you do it! [*Imploringly.*] Just *once* more, Dr. Herdal!

DR. HERDAL.

If I did, Hilda, my medical knowledge, slight as it is, leads me to the conclusion that I should in all probability burst.

HILDA.

[*Looks deeply into his eyes.*] So long as you burst *beautifully!* But no doubt that Miss Blakdraf——

DR. HERDAL.

You must believe in me utterly and entirely. I will do anything—*anything*, Hilda, to provide you with agreeable entertainment. I *will* swallow my own powder! [*To himself, as he goes gravely up to dispensary.*] If only the drugs are sufficiently adulterated!

> [*Goes in; as he does so, the* NEW ASSISTANT *enters the garden in blue spectacles, unseen . by* HILDA, *and follows him, leaving open the glass door.*]

SENNA.

[*Comes wildly out of drawing-room.*] Where is dear Dr. Herdal? Oh, Miss Wangel, he has discharged me—but I can't—I simply *can't* live away from that lovely ledger.

HILDA.

[*Jubilantly.*] At this moment Dr. Herbal is in the dispensary, taking one of his own powders.

SENNA.

[*Despairingly.*] But—but it is utterly impossible! Miss Wangel, you have such a firm hold of him—*don't* let him do that!

HILDA.

I have already done all I can.

[RÜBUB *appears, talking confidentially with*
MRS. HERDAL, *at gate.*

SENNA.

Oh, Mrs. Herdal, Rübub! The Pill-Doctor is
going to take one of his own preparations. Save him
—quick !

RÜBUB.

[*With cold politeness.*] I am sorry to hear it—for
his sake. But it would be quite contrary to professional etiquette to prevent him.

MRS. HERDAL.

And I never interfere with my husband's proceedings. I know *my* duty, Miss Blakdraf, if *others*
don't !

HILDA.

[*Exulting with great intensity.*] At last ! Now I
see him in there, great and free again, mixing the

powder in a spoon—with jam!'. . . . Now he raises the spoon. Higher—higher still! [*A gulp is audible from within.*] There, didn't you hear a harp in the air? [*Quietly.*] I can't see the spoon any more. But there is one he is striving with, in blue spectacles!

The New Assistant's Voice.

[*Within.*] The Pill-Doctor Herdal has taken his own powder!

Hilda.

[*As if petrified.*] That voice! *Where* have I heard it before? No matter—he has got the powder down! [*Waves a shawl in the air, and shrieks with wild jubilation.*] It's too awfully thrilling! My—*my* Pill-Doctor!

The New Assistant.

[*Comes out on verandah.*] I am happy to inform you that—as, to avoid accidents, I took the simple precaution of filling all the dispensary-jars with camphorated chalk—no serious results may be anticipated from Dr. Herdal's rashness. [*Removes spec-tacles.*] Nora, don't you know me?

HILDA.

[*Reflects.*] I really don't remember having the pleasure—— And I'm *sure* I heard a harp in the air!

MRS. HERDAL.

I fancy, Miss Wangel, it must have been merely a bee in your bonnet

THE NEW ASSISTANT.

[*Tenderly.*] Still the same little singing-bird! Oh, Nora, my long-lost lark!

HILDA.

[*Sulkily.*] I'm *not* a lark—I'm a bird of prey—and when I get my claws into anything—— !

THE NEW ASSISTANT.

Macaroons, for instance? I remember your tastes of old. See, Nora! [*Produces a paper-bag from his coat-tail pocket.*] They were fresh this morning!

" My, my Pill-doctor ! "

HILDA.

[*Wavering.*] If you insist on calling me Nora, I think you must be just a little mad yourself.

THE NEW ASSISTANT.

We are all a little mad—in Norway. But Torvald Helmer is sane enough still to recognise his own little squirrel again! Surely, Nora, your education is complete at last—you have gained the experience you needed ?

HILDA.

[*Nods slowly.*] Yes, Torvald, you're right enough *there*. I have thought things out for myself, and have got clear about them. And I have quite made up my mind that Society and the Law are all wrong, and that I am right.

HELMER.

[*Overjoyed.*] Then you *have* learnt the Great Lesson, and are fit to undertake the charge of your children's education at last! You've no notion how they've grown! Yes, Nora, our marriage will be a true marriage now. You will come back to the Dolls' House, won't you?

HILDA-NORA-HELMER-WANGEL.

[*Hesitates.*] Will you let me forge cheques if I do, Torvald?

HELMER.

[*Ardently.*] All day. And at night, Nora, we will falsify the accounts—together!

HILDA-NORA-HELMER-WANGEL.

[*Throws herself into his arms, and helps herself to macaroons.*] That will be fearfully thrilling! My —*my* Manager!

DR. HERDAL.

[*Comes out very pale, from dispensary.*] Hilda I *did* take the—— I'm afraid I interrupt you?

HELMER.

Not in the least. But this lady is my little lark,

and she is going back to her cage by the next steamer.

Dr. Herdal.

[*Bitterly.*] Am I *never* to have a gleam of happiness? But stay—do I see my little Senna once more?

Rübub.

Pardon me—*my* little Senna. She always believed so firmly in my pill!

Dr. Herdal.

Well—well. If it must be. Rübub, I will take you into partnership, and we will take out a patent for that pill, jointly. Aline, my poor dear Aline, let us try once more if we cannot bring a ray of brightness into our cheerless home!

Mrs. Herdal.

Oh, Haustus, if only we *could*—but why do you propose that to me—*now?*

Dr. Herdal.

[*Softly—to himself.*] Because I have tried being a troll—and found that nothing came of it, and it wasn't worth sixpence!

> [Hilda-Nora *goes off to the right with* Helmer; Senna *to the left with* Rubub; Dr. Herdal *and* Mrs. Herdal *sit on two of the galvanised-iron chairs, and shake their heads disconsolately as the Curtain falls.*

.

.

Printed by BALLANTYNE, HANSON AND CO.
London and Edinburgh.

www.ingramcontent.com/pod-product-compliance
Lightning Source LLC
Chambersburg PA
CBHW030734280326
41926CB00086B/1531